Hard Bargains or Weak Compromises?

Hard Bargains or Weak Compromises?

Reforming Britain's relationship with the EU

Brian Binley and Lee Rotherham

Civitas: Institute for the Study of Civil Society
London

First Published March 2015

© Civitas 2015
55 Tufton Street
London SW1P 3QL

email: books@civitas.org.uk

All rights reserved

ISBN 978-1-906837-68-6

Independence: Civitas: Institute for the Study of Civil Society is a registered educational charity (No. 1085494) and a company limited by guarantee (No. 04023541). Civitas is financed from a variety of private sources to avoid over-reliance on any single or small group of donors.

All publications are independently refereed. All the Institute's publications seek to further its objective of promoting the advancement of learning. The views expressed are those of the authors, not of the Institute.

Designed and typeset by
lukejefford.com

Printed in Great Britain by
Berforts Group Ltd
Stevenage, SG1 2BH

Slobodni I suvereni narodi zalogsu mira I svekolikog napretka

Free and sovereign people are the pledge of peace and entire progress

Message of Peace from Zagreb, St Thomas' Peace Garden, Birmingham

Contents

Authors	viii
Foreword	ix
Acknowledgements	xi
Executive Summary	xii
1 Nationhood and the EU	1
2 Regaining a Voice	8
3 Proper Procedure	13
4 Over the Sea	24
5 Money Still Matters	42
6 Cutting Loose	57
7 Planning	75
Conclusion	107
Appendices	110
Endnotes	131

Authors

Brian Binley entered Parliament after a successful business career. He set up two companies which now employ approaching 300 people. He first became actively involved in Party activity as a Young Conservative in 1959. He is MP for Northampton South, and is a member of the Business, Industry and Skills Select Committee as well as a member of the Council of Europe's Parliamentary Assembly. He was chosen to chair the Conservative Party's Parliamentary Enterprise Group, and also chaired a review into the decline of the high street. He has been elected to the 1922 Committee every year since 2006, and since 2010 has been its Treasurer. As a result he additionally has extensive experience serving on the Conservative Party Board. His work with Ruth Lea looking at the UK's relationship with the EU remains a critical document for students of the issue. In late 2014, he was co-author with Rotherham (and Lord Tebbit) of the *Spotter's Guide to Sound Government Policies*.

Lee Rotherham is an author, research consultant, and a warrant officer in the army reserves who has undertaken three tours of duty. At Westminster, he has advised three shadow foreign secretaries plus a number of other front benchers, and was Campaign Secretary for Conservatives Against a Federal Europe (CAFE) – an organisation which increasingly looks like it needs to come back out of stasis. He was also the 'chief of staff' to a delegate on the Convention on the Future of Europe, and ran Opposition Research for the 'No to AV' referendum campaign. As the EU campaigner at the TaxPayers' Alliance, he was responsible for the definitive audits of the CFP, CAP, ECHR and the CFSP. Co-author of the hit *Bumper Books of Government Waste*, he helped set the agenda over public spending excesses. Extensively published, some of his more recent works include *The EU in a Nutshell* (foreword by Dr David Starkey), *A Fate Worse Than Debt: A History of Britain's National Debt from Boadicea to David Cameron*, *Manning the Pumps: How to Salvage the Eurosceptic Credentials of the Conservative Party* (foreword by Sir Bernard Ingham), *The Discerning Barbarian's Guidebook to Roman Britain*, *The Discerning Gentleman's Guide to Travel in His Majesty's Fractious American Colonies*, and *The Sassenach's Escape Manual* (with a foreword by Sir Teddy Taylor). Two more historical tour guides are due out in 2015.

Foreword

Our membership of the European Union is at the top of the agenda of many Conservative MPs. It stays there despite the polling evidence and siren voices of those who like our current relationship telling us that Europe is not a big issue with voters. It is high up the list of Conservative MPs because the European Union now controls or influences so many aspects of our lives that are crucial issues with voters.

The last Conservative government in the 1980s and 1990s kept immigration to around 50,000 a year. The last Labour government allowed net migration to rise fivefold to around 250,000. The current government wants to get it back down, in line with the wishes of a majority of electors. Instead they have discovered that the UK no longer has the power to control her own borders, but has to accept as many people as wish to come from the rest of the EU.

Many people have complained for good reason about high energy prices. In recent years dear electricity has eaten into family incomes. Conservatives want us to enjoy cheaper energy, as the US does. That helps create more industrial investment and jobs, and leaves families with more money to spend on other things. Unfortunately, the EU's strict requirements on how much energy we generate from wind farms and other renewables means we are going to have to accept dearer electricity for many years.

Many people agree with the government that we need to get our budget deficit and borrowing down. As we try to do so, the EU pops up with demands for higher contributions from the UK. The UK government has sought to negotiate lower budgets, yet poor spending discipline and a waywardness over commitments means the EU comes back later in the year demanding money from us we cannot afford.

There are many more examples of important matters that come wholly or partially under the control of Brussels. People want their own UK government to be able to police our borders, look after our fishing grounds, make planning decisions, settle our spending and taxes, and ensure we have a plentiful supply of reasonably priced energy. Under current arrangements that and many other things are partially or wholly beyond parliament's authority.

Mr Cameron has rightly told us our present relationship with the EU does not work in the UK's interests. He has said he wishes to see a sovereign UK parliament capable of making the big decisions which matter to UK citizens. He has promised us a renegotiation of our relationship. I wish him well, and want to see him leading a Conservative majority government to bring this all about. More importantly I look forward to the referendum which follows the negotiation. If he has gained us a new relationship based on trade and political co-operation I will vote for it. If the negotiation falls short of restoring our authority over the things that matter I will vote to leave.

The referendum is a crucial part of the approach. It will be a clear signal to our EU partners, who may not be keen to negotiate another special deal for us, that if they cannot accommodate our wishes we might well leave. That means no more UK contributions to help pay for their budget, and no more automatic right for future migrants to come to the UK.

This pamphlet sets out some of the matters that the authors wish to see renegotiated. It is a good guide to the wide range of EU powers, and the degree of EU intervention in our national life. Readers including me will not agree with all of the detailed proposals, but the thrust is clearly right. We need the EU to do less as we go about restoring UK parliamentary control, so parliament can respond to the wishes of our electors.

I would sum up my suggestion for a negotiating aim as the restoration of UK ultimate control over important matters, so we can say to voters once again their parliament can respond to their wishes and get things done as they want. This pamphlet helps the case by reminding us of the range and complexity of the issues. I hope Ministers study it as they work out how to approach these crucial negotiations.

Rt Hon John Redwood MP

Acknowledgements

Thanks are due to David Moller, Anthony Scholefield, the Rt Hon John Redwood MP and all the staff at Civitas.

Note on the Title

The title for this book is taken from a speech by Sir Winston Churchill in 1950 on a peaceful European settlement:

> The first stage is to create a friendly atmosphere and feeling of mutual confidence and respect. Even a day's delay in working hard for this is a matter for regret. Once the foundation of common interest and solidarity of sentiment has been laid, it may well be that formal agreements would take the form, not of hard bargains or weak compromises, but of setting down on paper the living basic truths and thoughts which were in all minds. Then difficulties, at present insuperable, might well become irrelevant.
>
> Rt Hon Sir Winston Churchill, MP, Hansard, 28 March 1950

The same principles apply for how we start now to develop and renegotiate a friendly rearrangement of the continent today.

Executive Summary

- The UK is right to renegotiate its terms of association with the EU. Other countries fare better given their history, geography, regulatory burdens, and cross-border economies. But the terms serve us badly and are getting worse with time.

- The UK's own interests are no longer served by acting as the maligned brake that other capitals quietly depend on.

- Qualified Majority Voting (QMV) has changed the dynamics away from states stacking bartering chips from their vetoes. Meanwhile, the *acquis communautaire* and the growth of the European Court of Justice and European Parliament constantly pull the centre ground (to which consensus diplomacy defaults) away from us. Europe is now a conveyer belt of compromise.

- So *fundamental* treaty change is needed from any renegotiation, removing entire articles and titles as applied to the UK; we suggest a number but this deserves considerable technical study across government.

- Just tweaking individual directives leaves the enduring problems unaddressed and doomed to reappear.

- Achieving wide-ranging reform of the Lisbon Treaty – 'pimping the EU' as the UK would prefer to see it run, by revoking the *acquis* as applied to everyone – is not realistic. It is sensible to test the water diplomatically on this but without wasting time over it.

- A bilateral deal between the UK as one party and the rest of the EU as the corporate other could, however, address the UK's issues by removing the controversies from EU control.

- By definition, this will change our individual treaty terms and we will no longer be 'EU members' in the current sense. But vocabulary doesn't matter – the terms do.

EXECUTIVE SUMMARY

- There are two paths to achieving an identical end goal – major renegotiation while maintaining transitional access to the single market; or withdrawal then renegotiation from scratch. Both are viable routes to an end destination – a matter of deciding to follow either an M1 or an A1(M).

- Renegotiation as a route makes more economic and diplomatic sense - but only if negotiators have a genuine commitment to stripping out what's wrong, and in bulk.

- Failing that, withdrawal to the European Economic Area (EEA) while working on the small print of a new trade treaty would be an improvement on our current lot and the EU's inevitable long term direction: federalisation and stagnation.

- Delegates to the talks need to go retro-minimalist – to use the opportunity to start planning from a treaty of basic trade association, and think outwards from there. The onus should be on requiring civil servants to make the case for anything to be done in Brussels, not the reverse.

- The accompanying debate itself might prudently focus on the themes of:
  the sovereignty and accountability deficit;
  a holistic set of policies on the migrant-addicted economy;
  bullet-proofing the City;
  plugging the membership fees, waste, and Eurozone drag;
  reconfiguring access to global markets by understanding the costs that go with the 'single market' or even just the customs union option;
  and localism as a long term motor of managing where powers lie.

- Any treaty change is an opportunity, not an end in itself. All the red tape that can be stripped domestically, while retaining export compliance, then must be.

- Making a nugatory deal then managing to briefly sell it in a referendum would ruin any hope of significant EU reform for at least a generation. Indeed, all EU members would be losers. Moreover, UK withdrawal further down the line would become inevitable and far more messy.

- Meanwhile the 15 different types of EU deal that *already* exist need far greater official study and debate. That way we can review in which degree of Brussels orbit our national interest is best served, even with just looking at what is presently on the menu. Ministers should also honestly come to terms with what the Foreign and Commonwealth Office (FCO) already judged the Brussels end destination to be in the 1960s and 1970s; and repudiate it today.

- Finally, as the most important immediate step, we need a genuine wide-ranging cost-benefit analysis of the UK's membership and interests before we start negotiating.

1

Nationhood and the EU

The status quo is not an option

> **Bottom lines up front**
> - The Conservative policy of EU renegotiation is a debate leader in Westminster.
> - It will impact directly on manifestos and cannot be ignored even by those who politically oppose it.

The Conservatives have an objective: fixing the UK's relationship with the EU so that it works.

Conservative Party policy can be summarised as a three point plan. In the first instance, it involves a period of reflection and assessment, of consideration over where the balance of benefit lies in our terms. This has largely to date been associated with the Balance of Competences Review within government, and has found contributions now including this short publication adding to the mix.

Such additions are particularly crucial given the criticisms associated with the review to date, including charges that it has been partial, Whitehall-centred, unnecessarily cautious, and too reliant for input from those who benefit financially from the current EU system (lobbyists and EU-sponsored experts). Consequently the review has been not nearly critical enough of current flaws and costs and possible wider benefits of truly serious reform. In sum, it has fallen short in vision and substance. But we can still fix that.

The second phase in the Conservative timeframe that is yet to follow is one of renegotiation, which comes (provisionally) after the next General Election. The third and final element is a confirmatory – or repudiatory – referendum.

As a consequence, of the parties of government so far only the Conservative Party is addressing the issue of how the United Kingdom economically, politically and in treaty terms fits into the machinery of continental governance, in order to better explore what forms of looser association may work more effectively. Or, to put it another way as the Prime Minister has said:

> The biggest danger to the European Union comes not from those who advocate change, but from those who denounce new thinking as heresy. In its long history Europe has experience of heretics who turned out to have a point.
>
> And my point is this. More of the same will not secure a long-term future for the Eurozone. More of the same will not see the European Union keeping pace with the new powerhouse economies. More of the same will not bring the European Union any closer to its citizens. More of the same will just produce more of the same – less competitiveness, less growth, fewer jobs.
>
> And that will make our countries weaker not stronger.
>
> That is why we need fundamental, far-reaching change.[1]

The key phrase here is the last one. The Conservatives have to set out what 'fundamental, far-reaching change' actually consists of. The greatest difficulty may be in defining it to the public. A deal that generates minor tinkering will be disastrous for the EU, since it will demonstrate it is incapable of meaningful and necessary reform now or ever in the future. But actually endorsing such a deal would also then be catastrophic for the Conservative Party. It would suggest that it was never serious about meaningful change. It would indicate that the party is not a credible defender of the national interest. It would associate the Party directly with the guilty elements responsible for the salami slicing of our nation's sovereignty since the departure of Margaret Thatcher, and the slow puncture of our vital economic interests through Brussels and the Luxembourg Court since.

Other political parties have yet to fully align their positions with these aspirations. UKIP's is well known, and predicated upon what appears to be a less nuanced stance of straight-out withdrawal. Even here, however, there are naturally questions as to what would then be identifiable as topics for inclusion in talks that would then inevitably follow over trade and tariffs. Certainly there will be areas that the Commission and a number of remaining EU members would like to see put on the agenda as ongoing bilaterals. Labour currently appears to be fixed against any major renegotiation, but this could be overturned by any sudden Eurozone crisis and a Frankfurt-driven push for greater Eurozone integration. The current parliamentary delegate for the Greens was known as something of a Eurosceptic while an MEP. Even the Liberal Democrats appear to accept that the triggering of a popular vote through the Referendum Lock at some point may be a game-changer. We are only four elections in distance from when Sir Jimmy Goldsmith turned a referendum promise on Brussels into a manifesto pulper.

While the Prime Minister's pledge of a referendum at the point in writing is tactically tied to the current fortunes of just one party, strategically its consequences are more widely felt, and will become government's wider responsibility to implement should the Conservatives win the 2015 General Election.

So what, from the viewpoint of the proposer, is this all about?

Current objectives

Bottom lines up front

- The declared focus of renegotiation is on competitiveness, flexibility, a system that allows competences to be handed downwards, more power for national parliaments, and fairness for non-Eurozone members.
- These remain open to interpretation, not least over what powers should in fact be returned to national control.
- That list needs to be well-defined, wide-ranging, and to form absolute red lines.
- The instant we spot there is no prospect of changing the treaties for everyone (likely), we need to swiftly shift into renegotiating the treaty which governs our association instead.

The Prime Minister's 2013 Bloomberg speech identified five targets without – it needs to be underlined – excluding the possibility of there being any others. Let's review these in turn.

Firstly, there was *competitiveness*, expressed as meaning the further development of the single market. As an unquantified abstract, this is an achievable aim. It is, however, a long-term mission and likely to be tick-boxed after any negotiations by the simple and vacuous publication of a declaration of intent stating that it is an enduring aspiration of the Commission to push for this, just as it has supposedly been pushing for the last twenty years.

It is worth remembering though that this objective can also be achieved, and produce benefits, without actual EU membership. Opening up access to the EU's customs bloc can also be associated with advances in world trade terms and obligations, or as part of bilaterals. Single market affiliation is itself not even necessarily a must.

The competitiveness target is also associated with the reduction of red tape, to which we return later. It is important at this point to acknowledge that the Commission has a very poor track record on tackling bureaucratic burdens even when it itself acknowledges them as an issue. This means that getting a simple statement that the Commission accepts there is a problem is not enough to secure this as a negotiation 'win'. Past drives to cut red tape have seen the Commission effectively fake its level of activity by providing paltry lists of repealed legislation that amounted to little more than laws that had been superseded by later versions, or were patently out of date. An EU with an administrative budget and staffing levels that had been slashed to levels Francis Maude could achieve would be a more obvious indicator of true intent. The noisy Eurocrat unions would never stomach this, though.

The second target that has been set out involves *flexibility*. Essentially, this involves the EU formally recognising that a two-system Europe was a permanent fixture of the way Brussels operated (with a 'two-speed Europe' officially having parked its cars). This division has now become geologically fixed with the establishment of a single currency bloc to which the UK will, realistically, never accede. However, the practicalities of securing for instance the protection of non-Eurozone rights within a single-fit system are complex. It relies on one of two things happening to provide anything approaching a guarantee of security. The first is a ruling by the European Court of Justice that all states have equality of rights in how they are dealt with by the institutions, while also confirming separately that there is not an equality of obligations under human rights grounds. This is realistically an impossible mix; therefore the reality will be that it needs to be ensconced in the primary treaties themselves. Even then, if we follow this tack, in practice we will still operate in an informal second tier membership, since we are already seeing that non-Eurozone members have difficulty in getting their nominees considered as credible Commission candidates in a number of areas for which the country of origin enjoys an opt-out. It is correspondingly likely that informally, a British or Danish Commissioner will never hold a monetary or home affairs portfolio, which (despite the rules but in reality) also then creates a knock on effect on senior staffing in those Directorates-General as well.

The third target is that 'power must be able to flow back to member states, not just away from them': *Euro-devolution*. As David Cameron correctly observed, this was precisely what the Laeken Conference intended. That intent however was subverted within the very first week of the Convention on the Future of Europe, indicating once again that any deal including simply a statement of broad intent will not be worth the paper it is written on once personalities become involved in applying it.[2]

Actioning this restoration of powers is the single most important aspect of treaty change. It requires a clear hit list of competences that need to go back to the UK, to make our association with the EU work. There is a crucial rider to this.

It also requires accepting from the outset that if multilateral reform cannot be achieved by inserting opt-outs within the existing treaties, then the changes can only be achieved bilaterally, between the UK and the EU as distinct but associated blocs.[3] That means ending the current treaty and generating a special treaty of association, with trade access for the UK short of full membership, in which the contentious articles and titles are specifically excluded. So much of what the EU today does is not concerned with simple trade at all and carry financial burdens – politically-motivated rather than economically-rational bolt-ons.[4]

Before we get to that stage we need to have a crystal-clear perception of what our baseline terms need to be and what areas need to be cut. We address this later in this paper, but it needs now to be the subject of wide debate within parties, taking place in association with communities affected by EU legislation. Setting up an online wiki site would be a positive step for engagement.

The fourth target declared by the Prime Minister is that of *democratic accountability*, creating a greater role for national parliaments. The parliamentary red card trigger generated by the Treaty of Lisbon (more of an amber one in practice) was deliberately set at a near-impossible threshold, made even more difficult by the legislative timeframe, translation times, and inherent lack of communication between objecting parliamentarians. Attempts by *Eurosceptics* on the Convention to reduce the threshold were ignored and it is difficult to imagine these alternatives being any more popular now; but the proper threshold certainly should be that any single parliament should have the right to veto legislation, rather than try to rush around lobbying for an alliance that might at best delay a pernicious and unpopular law.[5] In short, the 'parliamentary reserve' should have force of law. What use otherwise is an MP who is instructed by a minister from another party they cannot vote against a law, or even a government minister who is ordered by a civil servant to sign off an EU document as there is no alternative allowed? As the Prime Minister noted:

It is national parliaments, which are, and will remain, the true source of real democratic legitimacy and accountability in the EU.

But that simply is not the way the system works. Nor can the Brits in the European institutions themselves act as a surrogate safeguard. Nationals in the Commission are legally obliged to be neutral, though inherently tend to be integrationist; British MEPs even acting in unison meanwhile make up under ten per cent of the total; British ministers in a world where QMV is the norm rather than the exception have just eight per cent of the vote.[6]

The fifth principle is that of *fairness*, ensuring that the rules don't discriminate particularly over Eurozone rules impacting on non-Eurozone countries. The example of the Exchange Rate Mechanism, of which the Prime Minister had a certain and unhappy first hand experience as a Special Adviser (SpAd), may help to dissuade us of being too optimistic of taking anything not expressly set out in treaty paragraphs at trust. A recent example is that of the misuse of the Disaster Clause, Article 222. Intended as a mechanism to share the burden in the event of a massive disaster or for coping with an unimaginable terrorist atrocity, it was instead applied to lumber member states with Eurozone liabilities. This is a particularly worrying demonstration that even apparently clearly expressed parts of the treaty are liable for abuse regardless of principles of fair play or the supposed existence of an impartial civil service or arbitration court.

From these five objectives though it's fair to state that any attempt to achieve them will not be a paltry exercise. As the Prime Minister accepted at Bloomberg:

> I have no illusions about the scale of the task ahead.
>
> With courage and conviction I believe we can achieve a new settlement in which Britain can be comfortable and all our countries can thrive.
>
> And when the referendum comes let me say now that if we can negotiate such an arrangement, I will campaign for it with all my heart and soul.

That last statement contains a conditional clause: it is dependent on the word 'if'. It relies upon a conditioned event, of achieving a new deal. But it is a critical mission and we need to get it right.

Speaking at the CBI's 2014 annual conference, the Prime Minister revisited these objectives and summarised them in the following terms;

> Now, I'm the politician who has the plan for that reform, who wants to see the single market safeguarded and not have us ordered around by the single currency countries. I want to make sure we belong to a Europe that is about a

common market and cooperation and not about an ever closer union and I want to belong to a Europe that addresses people's concerns, including concerns like immigration.

So the renegotiation policy as of late 2014 was confirmed as still that of securing continuing trade access; some manner of codifying an end state on European integration (notwithstanding the incessant rip tide pull of the ECJ), and a list of public concerns that need review. That list, though, still remains unspecified both in terms of its content and its direction.

Success will come in two forms. Either it will set a high bar that will be passed, meaning that this nation will be secure and restful in the terms of our partnership with Brussels; or it will set a high bar and not be met, in which case it will be the trigger for us to set out new terms of negotiation that are more clearly distinct from the current treaties, framing our relationship in a fresh document, in an unambiguous and equally positive and enduring way.

Failure does not take the form of a renegotiation that is rejected by a referendum. Failure is where the terms met are fraudulent. A thin bubble wrap deal that pops away over time will swiftly be seen as a sham by the British people, discrediting the Conservative Party, and undermining parliament itself. It will achieve the remarkable result of turning UKIP practically overnight into a party of governance. More importantly, it will sap the British constitution, society and economy as false fit terms try to badly mask an enduring seepage of powers to Brussels. Further reforms will be blocked for a generation and the system will ossify beyond redemption.

That's why we need to get the deal right; and why think tanks and experts need collectively to spell out what's bust, so that we can resolve what precisely needs to get fixed.

2

Regaining a Voice

Ham-stringing the outriders of integration

> **Bottom lines up front**
> - EU-funded campaigners, experts and lobbyists are also part of the gravitational pull of integration.

There is a further dynamic involved and that is the use of integrationist proxies.[1] The ECJ, like the other EU institutions, is dependent on outriders and front people to pull forward its agenda. EU-funded campaigners justify Commission engagement in areas national governments see as their own; prompt MEPs to seize terrain in areas of supposed public interest; and take governments or even the EU itself to court when they fail to be aggressive enough in agreeing with their agenda. To quote Professor Karen Alter:

> The European Commission knows that litigants will not self-organise. The Commission has actively sought out interlocutors so as to build a constituency that might support its efforts. [...] The Commission uses its power to propose legislation to mobilize domestic actors, and to keep previously mobilised actors interested in European Union politics.[2]

Even if we could trust the ECJ to remain neutral, we would have to neuter such taxpayer-funded euro-lobby groups by removing their funding in order to restore balance amongst the lobbyists seeking to overturn the UK's sovereign safeguards. This is an important objective in its own right and should be pursued anyway.

However, that still leaves us with issues such as the selection of the people within the ECJ itself. The institution by its very nature can only be skewed. Just as the European Commission recruits people who are disproportionately pro-European, and who have by the nature of the *concours* system been 'acclimatised' to the Brussels stratosphere, so too the very nature of the CVs required to be a candidate for Luxembourg judiciary eschews individuals jealous of the rights of what are to them inherently lower courts. This is not an indictment of them as people, but a plain fact of recruitment that obviously impacts upon their work: it is in this regard no different from the mechanics in play when recruiting for a panel manned by, say, gender equality professionals or global warming campaigners. Their findings will inevitably display professional bias.[3]

A quick review of the published backgrounds of current ECJ judges reveals former lecturers at the EU's teaching establishment, a past member of the Committee of the Regions, legal advisers and team leaders during treaty negotiations, external advisers to the Commission, Commission legal staffers, members of Commission think tanks and working groups, ministers responsible for legal issues during accession, Jean Monnet professors, drafters of the European Constitution, and members of the Strasbourg human rights commission. It is inevitable that most if not all have been recipient of EU grants either on training courses, conferences, or as part of their time spent heading up centres and associations of EU law. Many will have received EU funding in their academic careers. Inherently, the selection takes place from a pool infused with clear affiliation to the objectives of European integration: indeed, the mission depends on it.

Whatever it may achieve in terms of changing the treaties, and regardless of the merits of individuals (particularly those exposed to Common Law traditions and practices – and there are some on that list of current ECJ judges) Downing Street cannot hope to achieve reform of this élite on a sufficient scale to guarantee its interests if the treaties are modified in a partial, ambiguous, and disputed arrangement without solid legal bastions. Nudging individual clauses in existing treaties, or attempting to produce explanatory riders agreed in the Council of Ministers, will leave any deal at the mercy of the Luxembourg Court and will lead to its inevitable erosion. A political deal will not do: the treaty text itself needs a major, unambiguous overhaul.

Sovereignty within parliament

Bottom lines up front

- Any system that does not give parliament a veto will not work.
- The EU system does not allow this, but the EEA system does provide us with a model.

Part of the answer depends on finding agreement on some of the choke points and strangle holds that our democracy can exercise in a reasonable and reasoned manner. The problem has been that centralised national democracies were never designed to cope with the European way of doing business.[4] Parliamentarians are merely the vavasours and petty vassals who are instructed by their local magnates to do the imperial bidding. They can question but not challenge what is passed down from a foreign capital.

This emasculation is most evident in the role of the Select Committees. The European Scrutiny Committee's Report on reforming scrutiny procedures in 2013 ran, not surprisingly, to three volumes.[5] It was also long overdue, in an area long left neglected by previous governments (perhaps out of embarrassment at the inability to provide any enduring fixes unilaterally). In addition to some useful recommendations that would increase transparency at least, it valuably explores what the minimum criteria need to be when setting out the parliamentary red card principle.

We can summarise them as follows. In the first instance, it is not enough to depend on creating a parliamentary blocking minority. Consultation with other parliaments should *follow* a red card, not be used to try (we suppose, often forlornly) to generate one. The Committee goes on:

> We further conclude that parallel provision should be made to enable a decision of the House of Commons to disapply parts of the existing *acquis*. This, we acknowledge, would require an Act of Parliament to disapply the European Communities Act 1972 in relation to specific EU legislation. There have been several Private Members' Bills over recent years endorsing the principle of disapplication which have sought to achieve this, and amendments to the same effect were proposed in both Houses to the Legislative and Regulatory Reform Bill in 2006, which were whipped by the then official opposition.

Essentially, the Committee is asking that the government accept the 'notwithstanding' principle as a fundamental in the UK applying EU law.

We can look at this from two vantage points: future law, and past law. Future law first.

This might be considered an impossible breach of EU membership obligations – and indeed it is. But it *is* fully compliant with the treaty format that accompanies membership of the EEA, where national parliaments and national governments exercise a right of veto to stop individual EU laws or regulations applying to themselves.[6] So, providing the terms of UK association with the EU were changed on a fundamental level, this is an achievable objective. It does mean moving away from the treaties as they currently stand.

In terms of past law, it is an understatement to say that it is an innovation amongst member states to try to remove *acquis*. The point of the *acquis* is for it to remain *acquired* as a permanent foundation, like some Middle Eastern *Tell* – an archaeological mound where buildings are ever being built upwards upon their predecessors. Such an approach is not, as it happens, an innovation for Conservative front benchers; and the Prime Minister's aspiration to restore powers to national control is merely fulfilling this parliamentary objective by diplomatic means.[7] The difference is that parliament is seeking to confirm that it has the authority to revoke individual directives and similar forms of legislation with which it disagrees, and in which there is no further international treaty obligation.

As the Committee itself recognises, the practicalities of this approach are extremely complex. It depends first and foremost on restoring unanimity in the Council and injecting what amounts to a parliamentary veto on the UKREP vote before it is cast. The former is achievable; the latter, given the state of European integration, is extremely unlikely. One can of course try. But realistically, negotiators should be alert to the reality that restoring sovereignty and accountability means stepping back from QMV. In turn, that means a total rethink of the UK's association terms and moving from the universal and multilateral format of the treaties in which we currently stand.

A critical failing

Bottom lines up front

- Democracy suffers from this deficit.
- It was a mistake to create MEPs rather than keep them as visiting MPs. But that can't now be fixed.

Why is this issue of sovereignty important? Simply, it is the lifeblood of democracy. Without the power to change bad conditions by reversing bad decisions, alleviating suffering, and overturning unfortunate case law, parliament is nothing. It has the equivalent force and meaning of a council debating a motion on international affairs. In turn, such toothlessness fosters public despair and is the surrogate for extremism. Thanks to being outside of the Eurozone we are some way off that unhappy place yet. But there is a compounded sense of outrage every time poor decision making in Brussels affects livelihoods in a member state.

A local slaughterhouse might be closed due to extra administrative burdens, adding extra stress to the animals. Or farmers might be lumbered with extra bills in hard times through having to dispose of fallen livestock in a manner best suited for lab technicians. But no-one is ever held responsible for failure.

This is as much due to the physical distance of the original legislators, as to the ambiguities arising from a system of gold plating where no one can determine which bits have been subjected to the Whitehall jeweller. But it means that scandals do not impede the culprit's career – though of course they can maul the minister who subsequently finds himself carrying the can.

This is particularly true when the media and the Opposition (who may even have been in office when the legislation was originally drafted) fail to make the connection between a decision and its ultimate EU source. The reluctance to dredge rivers that are prone to flooding is one recent example, where critics who blamed the minister failed to link apparent departmental inaction with guiding EU legislation encouraging flood plain diversity which added costs to dredging by reclassifying mud as industrial waste. The scale and obfuscated nature of the problem is such that we are almost tempted to invite any reader to pick a scandal of the past decade and try not to find an EU directive that has not caused or exacerbated it. Even if he finds one, it will be a policy area the Commission has probably expressed an interest in moving into.

Parliamentary accountability, and the restoration of some form of blocking power to parliament, is central to the deal on fixing this. The very system of law making in Brussels encourages this disconnect. Socialist and EPP group leaders historically get together behind closed doors and barter laws over a croissant. That might be a little more difficult to stitch up these days, but the torrent of hundreds of amendments that get voted on during Plenary is such that no one really understands what they are voting on other than the directing whip, and then only because he has a written prompt. Even the most contentious of votes goes unrecorded unless a political group makes a formal request to put something on the record. In February 2014, it was agreed at least that final votes in committees would be put on the record; but it's still left on the voting record for matters such as whether to adopt the contentious new Commission President a matter of conjecture. So we will never know the full list of which British MEPs for example were amongst those who also endorsed his appointment despite the comments of their respective party leaders back home (unless their political opponents snitch!)

3

Proper Procedure

Repairs in Brussels

> **Bottom lines up front**
> - The European Council system has serious flaws.
> - It encourages FCO pessimism and acquiescence in salami slicing.

One aspect that might be more readily fixed by applying direct parliamentary oversight lies in the European Council's way of doing business. Much of the trading takes place between members of the national Representations, of which UKREP is merely one. This is no different from any diplomatic setting. Where the system starts to fall down though is over A and B Points, since this allows bad laws to get through on the nod.

A Points are areas where agreements have been reached between officials, and the subject matter is held (not necessarily correctly) to be uncontentious. *B Points* require ministerial discussion. *Starred B Points* require ministerial batting. Some also refer to *False B Points* which are A Points deferred because of domestic political controversy. On top of this there are Points raised for information purposes only and which need no ministerial approval.

What is remarkable about this system is, firstly, the volume of material agreed as A Points. Indeed, it is the preferred mechanism, since it supposedly removes the scope for political argument as all civil service parties have signed the issue off. In practice though, it merely defers the problem to a later point, beyond which the minister can no longer block it and where it becomes potentially a much bigger political issue (just one that the staff in Brussels don't have to deal with any more). Much depends on the quality and attentiveness of the individual minister, who will almost certainly never set foot in a working meeting in his life.[1]

The second astonishing aspect is that A Points don't necessarily get carried across to the next relevant meeting, but to the next ministerial meeting. This means ministers may be agreeing on complex issues that have absolutely nothing to do with their brief. In May 2014 for example, the UK's Minister for Culture signed off on a report on auditing EU finances, a budget for Libyan border mission, and a Council policy on transparency. In June, the attending Lord Chancellor and Home Secretary between them also signed off changes to insolvency regulations, approved changing the nature of part of the ACP budget which carried significant implications on long-term policy direction, accepted a policy commitment over disaster relief, agreed to include a new social element to the EEA agreement, acknowledged (yet did not develop) a Court of Auditors' critique of the CAP, and instructed the Commission to draft a law on migrating wild animals.

This approach of course suits the national civil servants, who must be ecstatic at the resultant commanding role they play in our law making. Never has the manifesto been made so decisively in Whitehall and other chanceries of Europe. Such a mechanism neatly reduces the amount of awkward potential interference from ministers and speeds up policy making. But it is not accountable; nor is speedy law making of itself inherently a good thing.

We might have some measure of confidence if we knew that delegated staff were widely minded to oppose salami slicing. We do not intend to accuse senior FCO staff of lacking grit: anecdotally, we have heard good things of some senior individuals. But it does seem that, in contrast with a number of officials in other departments (particularly the Treasury, who do like to keep their money), historically as a collective they appear to lack élan, fortitude, resolve, and – frankly – concern. On a psychological level, too many civil servants appointed to positions of key responsibility relating to the EU were so advanced in going native in their *collectivisme* they practically didn't have British nationality to start with: they have been either fellow travellers in the European project, or content to paddle on any current that heads in that direction without excessively pondering it.

It is also a key sin that's been tolerated for too long, to view a half bad compromise as an improvement on a bad one, and a half-surrender as a negotiating success. Brussels operates over the long term, adding concessions consecutively. A half-surrender merely delays the surrender of the remainder at a later stage, and makes the ultimate loss seem less significant when it finally happens. Unless Westminster and Whitehall take a long-term view of how the EU operates, they will fail to appreciate what each individual agreement and surrender of powers actually means.

The FCO line on the EU remains one of managing decline rather than accepting Margaret Thatcher's assertion that we can and must do better. Damage limitation is about taking a pasting in order to avoid taking a pounding, when we should be avoiding taking both. Realistically, the immediate solution probably means bringing more people into UKREP from other parts of government, and in particular the Treasury. It also probably means generating a higher turnover of staff in EU-associated posts and it being a smaller portion of any individual's career, so the department moves away from producing a professional EU cadre.

The UKREP system needs a massive overhaul and as an area under direct Council remit, the management of council business can notably can be achieved without renegotiation – it could even be carried out to some extent unilaterally by injecting parliamentary oversight deeper into UKREP's workings and the management of A Points.

Fixing the democratic deficit

A quick review of three case studies can help establish where key fracture lines lie.

CASE STUDY 1: Bombay Duck.

Problem: Poor drafting/planning at Brussels.

Summary: A dozen tons of sun-dried Indian bummalo fish were exported annually to the UK. This was subject to a number of EU import requirements, including health certification and fumigation certification. In 1995, the Commission decided that locally-supplied health certification was insufficient and would need to be replaced by a Communities variant. This caused friction as it added extra costs to a very localised and small scale industry. In 1997, a ban on shrimp and squid following a genuine health issue in the fisheries was extended to the Bombay Duck fishermen, though they were from different fishing communities and the Commission had received no data on any health issues with this foodstuff. When the subject was reviewed by the Commission, it decided that exemptions would be permitted to certified establishments signed off by health inspectors, which was both costly and impractical for more distant villages. The small scale of the exports meant that the fishery, and therefore the product, was now unviable even with subsequent Commission concessions. MAFF, the precursor to DEFRA, took the position of keeping a low profile. The issue was only resolved because one company was finally found to take on the costs of being a certified packer.

Overview: A classic case of a distant Commission adding unnecessary regulatory burdens by irrelevant macromanagement, often seen by UK farmers and fishermen.

Resolution: Restore oversight to parliament along the entire food chain, which has the added advantage of starting to address the issue of how horse meat can enter UK supermarkets illicitly because it has been falsely certified using EU certification processes that are essentially beyond DEFRA's purview.

CASE STUDY 2: Package Travel Directive.

Problem: MEP gold plating.

Summary: An ongoing issue at the time of writing. The Commission had put forward a draft law intended to provide greater protection to holidaymakers. MEPs then put forward amendments. Critics within the tourism business suggest that these added legal uncertainty, loaded costs to travel agents that are actually the business of the airlines (notably on managing the impact of business failure), while ensuring that non-EU domiciled suppliers gain a competitive advantage.

Overview: One of sadly many instances where clueless lawmakers are lobbied by third parties, tinker with legislation they don't understand, agree to a muddled political compromise, and generate a draft or an amendment that others then have to fix.[2]

Resolution: Restoration of UK ultimate control over law making.

CASE STUDY 3: Examples of UK civil servants gilding the lily.

Problem: UK gold plating.

Summary: See Annex C for key examples cited by UK business.

Overview: Whitehall too readily is allowed to add unnecessary extra costs and go beyond what is needed under EU law.

Resolution: All EU-based legislation should be printed on distinct coloured paper in parliament. All European legislation must, excepting exceptional circumstances, be separately introduced rather than bolted on to other material or vice versa. All such legislation must demonstrate original departmental and Commission costings, the costings of the UK form of the legislation, and account for the difference as part of an obligatory part of the explanatory memorandum. This should be further associated with any cost-benefit analysis supplied, which must be reasoned.

Excessive latitude

> **Bottom lines up front**
> - The treaties contain legal holes that need to be plugged.

Other areas in need of tightening within the treaties are what are familiarly known as the 'rubber articles' (more widely familiar under the old pre-Lisbon numeration, Articles 94, 95 and 308[3]). These are blank slate articles that were originally designed to provide cover for unforeseen problems which may have arisen in the early stages of the creation of the single market. Where all member states could agree, the EU could be given the competence to do something not otherwise covered in the treaties. While this may have been a convenient ad hoc arrangement, the continued existence of such provisions has generated long term difficulties, not least where the Commission might interpret subsequent rights as automatically following on from the original grant.[4]

Under the Treaty of Lisbon, a safeguard was added: the Commission is now bound to draw the attention of national parliaments to their use. Yet there is no additional power for any assembly to do anything about it, excepting the European Parliament whose unreliability as a safeguard we can obviously predict. But this is not a new consideration, with the European Scrutiny Committee identifying it as an issue of concern in 2007.[5] One observation made by the Committee in particular demonstrates that the unanimity principle is not simply by itself a useful guarantor of the sovereign rights of parliament:

> We, and our predecessors, have identified some proposals for legislation for which Article 308 was cited as the legal base but which, in our opinion, had no or no substantial connection with the operation of the common market. For example, in 2006 the Commission, citing the Article as the legal base, proposed a draft Decision which would, among other things, provide for assistance from member states and the EC to third countries in the event of a major emergency outside the geographical area of the Community. We questioned whether Article 308 would provide a lawful legal base for the provision of assistance outside the Community if no connection could be shown to the operation of the common market. The government told us, however, that it considered the use of Article 308 to be acceptable because, in its view, it is not necessary that

"every proposal under Article 308 should relate in a narrow and restrictive sense to the operation of the common market". There was support from no other member state for the view that the Article was not appropriate. We remained unpersuaded by the government's view and drew the arguments to the attention of the House.

The Whitehall legal view seemingly remains that the rubber articles can be applied more widely than simply on trade: the list of areas to which they have been applied confirms this. Exacerbating matters further is the fact that the ECJ considers itself the ultimate arbiter of competences.

Consequently, on this issue the only enduring safeguard to the long term sovereign interests of this country must be to solder shut what amounts to a leaking stopcock. Either these articles must be deleted or expressly disapplied completely by treaty change, or else parliament must gain clear right of repeal over anything passed using them.[6]

If there remains any doubt of the need to restore explicit parliamentary supremacy to the EU treaties, these mechanisms may be usefully contrasted with systems which apply in other trade blocs.

Alternative models and lessons

> **Bottom lines up front**
>
> - Most other international trading associations are not integrationist, but cooperative.
> - They show the ECJ-run system to be excessive.
> - The comparison demonstrates the political intent for the EU and parts of Latin America to politically integrate over time.

Tellingly, it is only those international institutions that aspire to their own continental union that mimic the integrating dynamic of the ECJ. The Court of the Andean Community is an exemplar in copying the proactive ECJ format, though the Quito Court has a long way to go before it catches up with the competences covered by Luxembourg. Mercosur – with which it seems likely to ultimately merge – is a more prominent formalised customs union, and as such has adopted a legalistic approach to settling trade questions.[7] It was originally more of a free trade zone but has increasingly taken the integrationist approach. However, even here, member states continue to push for unilateral Free Trade Agreements (FTAs) with other countries and trading blocs. More free trading countries such as Chile have preferred to adopt an association status with their neighbours rather than full membership, since that allows them freedom of manoeuvre. It's for this precise reason that the Chilean experience, within the context of the several assimilationist blocs being pushed in South America, deserves wider study.

In contrast with the integrationist governments of Latin America, trading blocs whose function is to cover trade and not aspire to underpin political union are quite capable of adopting an approach that distinguishes between the sovereignty of the domestic legislators and the actual trade disputes themselves. ASEAN's charter, which came into force in 2008, explicitly highlights the protection of national sovereignty from its preamble onwards. So far from being associated with any court, the management format is so laid back it doesn't even specify how precisely it reaches its decisions beyond that it will typically be done by consensus.[8] It has a staff of around 260, a hundredth of that employed in Brussels, and fewer than the number employed by the Commission's Communications Directorate General alone.

NAFTA falls between the two models, but lies firmly in the multinational rather than integrationist approach. Disputes are first reviewed in the relevant working groups. If this fails, disputes are settled by arbitration according to the relevant section of the treaty, with Chapter Nineteen covering dumping and countervailing duties and Chapter Twenty of the treaty covering interpretation of the treaty itself. This latter is central, and operates in a manner not unlike WTO provisions. Significantly, North American legislators have moved away from extending this model, instead preferring further use of bilaterals, as they have found even this mechanism unresponsive in an age of high technology and internet sales.[9]

Thus we observe that there are very different models covering different models of trade associations. We shouldn't be surprised at this, given the sheer number of regional trading agreements in play. ACP, ACS, ALADI, Andean Community, APEC, APTA, ASEAN, BAFTA (now redundant), BSEC, CAFTA-DR, CARICOM, CELAC, CEMAC, CER/ANZCERTA, CIS, COMESA, EAC, EAEC, ECO, ECOWAS, IBSA, GCC, GSTP, MERCOSUR, MSG, NAFTA, Pacific Community, PATCRA, SAARC, SADC, SPARETECA, UNASUR, and WAEMU agreements differ from each other, but largely go for a court of arbitration rather than an arbitrary court. So even if we could, impossibly, shut down the ECJ overnight, we should not fear its removal as an essential adjunct of any trade association.

What is crucial, however, is that any significantly looser treaty agreement that applies to the UK should be policed not by the ECJ, but by the EFTA Court. This is the relevant authority providing legal oversight to the EEA Agreement for those countries that are not EU members: issues covering EU members remain governed by the ECJ. The EFTA Court was deliberately chosen by EEA members rather than the ECJ or a combined (minority EEA membership) option, on the basis that it is far more alert to sovereignty issues, and focuses more on genuine trade matters rather than extending the remit of other, associated competences. It is not an absolute safeguard of course, not least given the principles of indirect effect, but it is a considerable improvement.[10] It has to pay due account of new ECJ case law, but not slavishly. Meanwhile the ECJ has for its part also accepted that to preserve homogeneity it needs to do likewise with EFTA-EEA rulings. So, even if we stick with the existing legal framework, we have a choice in determining how we want our judicial reviews to function.[11]

The de-internationalisation of Britain

Bottom lines up front

- EU membership weakens the UK's international position.
- The UK surrenders its veto to the Commission at the UN coal face, and swaps it for QMV at the later Brussels coal heap.
- Regaining sovereignty from Brussels allows ministers to limit red tape burdens at their source.

Part of the problem with the sovereignty issue is that of double invisibility. Few people have an understanding or awareness of the process and progress made in international fora. The UK's diplomats are engaged in countless meetings in the UN and other world and regional bodies, setting the standards that then subsequently get translated into national law. There is a low level of direct accountability in this. Moreover, these roles are increasingly being subsumed by the European Commission as it asserts its legal rights as the lead or sole intermediary at these meetings.[12]

As a result, in areas where the UK does not enjoy the sole or any remaining treaty competence, it is down to the Commission or to the EU's External Action Service to take the national chair, argue a position, and cast the vote.

A simple list of how this arrangement was already standing in 2012 should suffice to make this point. It is, tellingly, extremely long and a summary of some key aspects can be found in Annex D.

The Brussels system peculiarly weakens national governments at the true coal face. It operates under the false pretence of providing a stronger negotiating hand, in a global system that in reality operates under consensus. Regaining the UK negotiating chair and veto from Brussels on any issue means getting a *stronger* negotiating hand in world trade fora outside of the customs union.

Subsequent to any talks, agreements then have to be transcribed into national law. This is often the source of EU law, which then is transcribed into domestic law or becomes directly applicable there.

It also – and this is a critical point – means, however, that EU negotiations are often merely discussions about how best to package decisions that have already been made by the Commission elsewhere. So actually restoring any given competence to national control is far more significant than one might think. It is actually about returning power to national governments to negotiate directly at the original drafting meetings. If the tinkering meetings are subject to QMV, the fundamental international meetings overwhelmingly remain places where a country can apply its veto.

The peculiarity of the system is such that Scandinavian diplomats from EU members reveal that they are not above badgering their Norwegian colleague at such international meetings to attempt to block a pernicious part of a world deal, since they themselves have no power if the Commission delegate is not interested.

A couple of examples here may suffice. EU Regulation 1102/2008 was the consequence of a decision to ban the export of metallic mercury and associated compounds 'to significantly reduce the global mercury supply.' It further sets out processes relating to its safe storage. At no point in the Regulation text does it mention anything other than EU decision making. It does, however, declare that 'Mercury releases are recognised as a global threat that warrants action at local, regional, national and global level,' hinting at something deeper going on, and reference a *Community Strategy Concerning Mercury*. It turns out on closer review that this is driven by discussions ongoing at the United Nations Environment Programme (UNEP), based on a specific global programme drafted at UN level in 2003.

Again, we might consider how the United Nations' Globally Harmonised System on the classification and labelling of chemicals (GHS) came about. This will be familiar to drivers as the pictogram system that can be found on tankers containing dangerous chemicals, though there is more to it than this. The back history forms part of a long line of European legislation stretching back to the Dangerous Substances Directive 67/548/EEC in 1967. This later developed into CHIP, the Chemicals (Hazard Information and Packaging for Supply) Regulations, grounded on two separate directives – the Dangerous Substances Directive (No. 67/548/EEC) and the Dangerous Preparations Directive (No. 99/45/EC). But after three decades of legislation, Community rules were now beginning to differ significantly from practice elsewhere on the continent. The result was that GHS was agreed at UN level to create a more uniform system.

As it happens, the end result of the negotiations was something based largely on the existing EU one. But for the non-EU negotiators, GHS is a voluntary agreement rather than a law. Across the EU however it was transposed into EU law as European Regulation (EC) No 1272/2008: the European Regulation on Classification, Labelling and Packaging of Substances and Mixtures (CLP Regulation).

The CLP rules are directly enforceable in EU states and thus did not have to be transposed into UK law by parliament. DEFRA estimated the cost of these changes to include hits to UK business from stock losses, staff training, potential 'classification inflation' of existing chemicals, relabelling, and IT changes.

The departmental audit declined to suggest any ballpark figure for the costs (or indeed the benefits). Tellingly, however, it observed that 'These differences between CLP and the GHS that may be adopted by non-EU countries may limit the benefits to international trade predicted for GHS and CLP' – in other words, non-EU countries were going to run their systems in a way without so much red tape.[13] This also made a nonsense of having a standard UN agreement in the first place.

Some statistics on the EU's international infrastructure may also help demonstrate the ongoing shift in power. Excluding Commission staff seconded as 'internal diplomats' to EU countries, EU diplomats operating under the External Action Service (EAS) rubric numbered 3,417 as at 2013 – making it larger than that of most individual member states.[14] This can be contrasted to the size of the diplomatic corps of other emerging powers; India has around 930, and Brazil 1,200. The EAS target is around 5,500, which will by then put it on a staffing par with Germany, France or the UK.

Conversely, Brussels itself is increasingly being seen as the go-to point for deal-making rather than necessarily to national capitals (certainly, the smaller ones).

The list of diplomats accredited to the EU as of mid-November 2014 stands at 238 pages. This excludes those from member states. Even the Cook Islands has a full-time delegate. Benin has 11 people accredited; the United States, 47; China, 74.

So much for the 'we are stronger because of the pooling of sovereignty' argument. Restoring any given power to national control is actually a treaty multiplier, since it allows that country to deal with legislative problems far higher upstream in the drafting process. UK diplomats will be able to set forward the national position much earlier in the process, months if not years before the EU comes to debate how to implement international agreements its own diplomats have been tasked with agreeing to. Critically, this is also the phase at which unanimity is required. Currently, the UK is largely confined to a QMV discussion on broad ranging direction before an international agreement is reached, then a QMV discussion on how to minimise the damage it faces in implementing it. It should be common sense that it is more advantageous to have a veto at the initial drafting phase, and then the ability to turn that into UK law in a manner best suited for our own particular domestic environment.

This is another reason why the renegotiation talks need to approach the sovereignty issue by repatriating sections of the treaty, and whole competency areas, rather than just attempting to fix isolated problems through changing the wording of a single sentence in an individual law.

4

Over the Sea

The immigration hand grenade

> **Bottom lines up front**
>
> - A political consensus has finally emerged recognising the issue exists, but emerging policies so far have failed to be wide-ranging and ambitious enough.
> - By definition there must be an annual immigration level that is 'too high', even if one can debate the actual level.
> - Government policy needs to consider skills, need and surplus. It cannot do so thanks to a core aspect of EU membership.
> - Failure to address public immigration concerns would carry immensely serious social dangers.

The UK has surrendered control over its borders. The decision to opt out of the Schengen Agreement leaves us with the illusion of power, but in reality the simple expediency of waving a burgundy passport reduces the ability of the state's lieutenants to intervene.[1]

David Cameron, in his November 2014 'JCB Speech', identified his priorities in what ground needed moving in this field.[2]

These comprised four elements. The first was an increase in power to deport people, and to refuse readmission. The second was a reduction in obligations to provide state support to EU jobseekers arriving without a firm job offer (with unstated ties in to ECHR reform, committed to previously). The third covered workers from future EU states, for which free movement would not apply (already policy, and obviously not affecting current member states). Finally, there was a commitment to introduce a residency time lapse for right to claim tax credits, child benefit and social housing.

Is this sufficient? The scale of the issue was certainly clear. Even as he answered questions, Mr Cameron admitted that currently four out of five new jobs created in London were not going to unemployed British nationals, and one in three nationally.

But a central acknowledgement was that such a new deal would require treaty change. That being the case, if the treaties are going to be reopened anyway, do these proposals alone suffice in correcting the problems, or is something more substantive and wide-ranging needed?

Let's begin with first principles. The ability to limit immigration is an important one. In pure abstract, this is indisputable. Clearly, a policy that would introduce the figure of one net migrant is not excessive and is manageable; a policy that introduced say 50 million would patently be unmanageable. The question therefore is not one of essential principle, but where the balance lies.

We can correspondingly look at the issue from two vantage points: the economic, and the social. From the latter aspect, the primary determinant is that of social cohesion. At what point do the existing inhabitants of this country take umbrage at the number of migrants in their midst who have arrived in such numbers that they have no incentive, need or capability to integrate (for instance, by learning the language)? This then acts as the fuel for hostility between divergent social and ethnic groups. From an EU perspective, culturally and historically as well as in terms of faith, these differences are perhaps less marked for EU migrants, particularly given the prevalence of English as a taught second language in many of these states.

The fact that tensions do exist in certain parts of the country of high migration, however, does demonstrate that there is a key identity conflict that accompanies the economic question. Bluntly put, where immigrants provide only a limited boon to the economy but are seen to be taking a local's job is where opinions over EU immigration start to harden.

Correspondingly, we need to be mature and exact when discussing the economics around migration. The campaign group MigrationWatch has conducted some very useful audits that have palpably undermined some rather shaky figures underpinning the Whitehall economics.[3] What is clear from these is that mere dint of presence is not sufficient for an additional migrant to add wealth to the UK economy in significant extent. Aside from such issues as wiring wages overseas rather than spending it in the local economy, there are both direct and indirect costs over health care and schooling provision (migrants are likely to be younger and fitter, but more liable to have children), translation services, social security and so forth. Then there is population density affecting quality of life and also economic efficiency, for instance by impacting upon transport networks or pushing up housing prices.

There are then a host of variables such as the impact of any (not necessarily immigrant) transient workforce on the local environment, or multiple residency arrangements surplus to housing design and council regulations. Tenancy vagaries and transitory rootlessness can be exacerbated further by genuine socio-cultural differences. Examples cited by annoyed constituents can include differing expectations of what constitutes acceptable late night noise; a lack of awareness of council rules and neighbourly norms in the disposal of household refuse; or not following UK legal practices by according a low priority to getting expensive car insurance. These sorts of differences have an economic cost in various forms but are also what fray community relations most.

Furthermore when judging optimal levels, we need to distinguish between skills, need, and surplus. We'll return to this in a moment. But essentially, the problem at its heart is that of the low skilled economy. The free movement of workers as permitted under EU rules means that the UK has lost control of the supply side of its workforce. This would not be an issue, but for the fact that it is subsidising its own native workforce to remain unemployed and our long-term uncompetitiveness by hiring in outside labour. This may be advantageous to the productivity of the companies in these areas, but it is disadvantageous to the taxpayer who has to effectively subsidise them by dole payments, while the UK workers affected fail to better themselves and rise up the employment ladder.

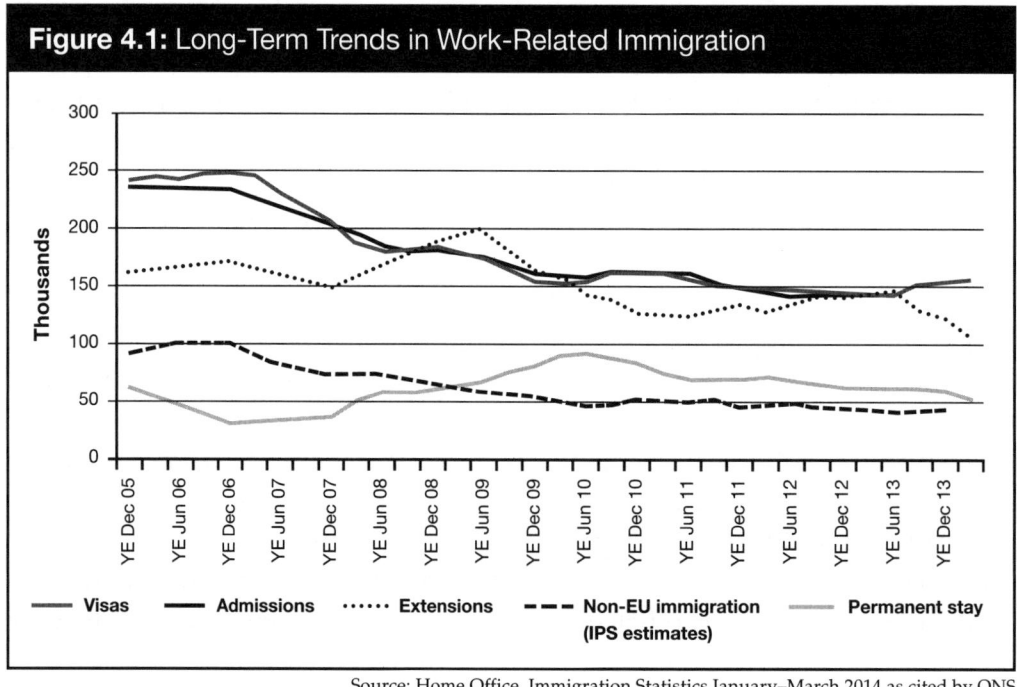

Figure 4.1: Long-Term Trends in Work-Related Immigration

Source: Home Office, Immigration Statistics January–March 2014 as cited by ONS

Some graphics may help to put these concerns into perspective. Figure 4.1 shows a levelling off of long term work-related visa stays. Around one third of visas issued are from India, followed by one tenth from each of Australia and the United States. One in three recipients of skilled work visas stay permanently. Around one in three of such extensions also go to Indian nationals. Chinese nationals get more extensions to stay, seemingly from students once they complete their studies, but not indefinitely.

This can be compared with the award of study sponsored visas in Figure 4.2. Reforms in the accreditation systems used by schools to clamp down on bogus language colleges have demonstrably had an effect.

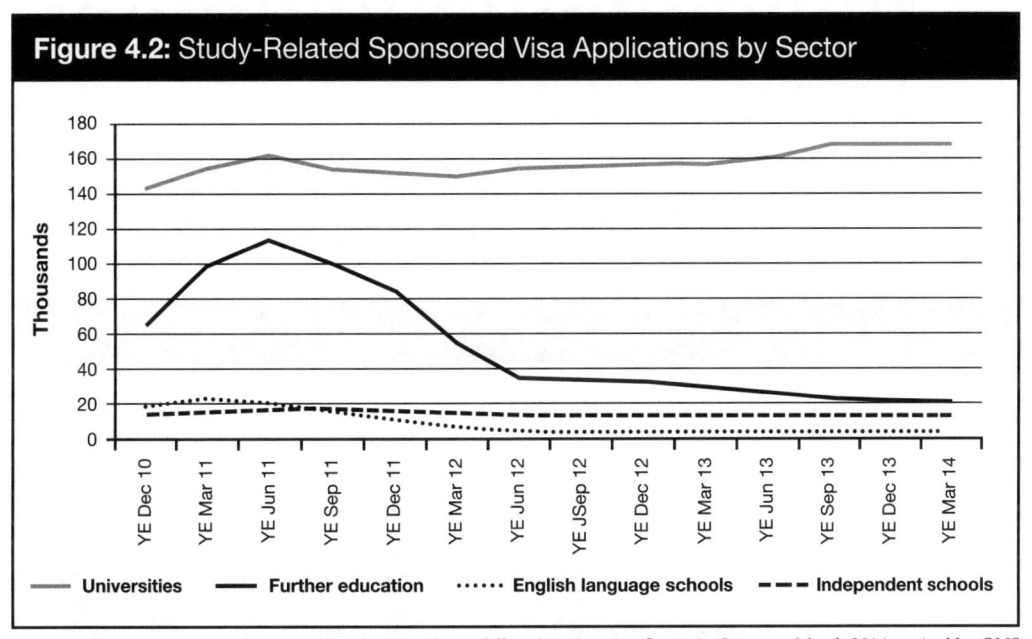

Figure 4.2: Study-Related Sponsored Visa Applications by Sector

Source: Home Office, Immigration Statistics January–March 2014 as cited by ONS

Figure 4.3 covers family migration. This remains a weak spot in the UK's migration system, not least as many successful immigrants have large families in their country of origin to whom they are potentially inclined to extend backing, bringing them over to the UK as well (an alternative mechanism historically is that of preferential employment, such as a taxi firm owner not employing locally, but instead bringing over a relative on a visa).

What we can see from these graphs and others like them is that some small progress has been made on attempting to reduce gross migration figures. Yet the net result remains a high level of permanent immigration, as Figure 4.4 demonstrates.

Figure 4.3: Long-Term Trends in Family Immigration

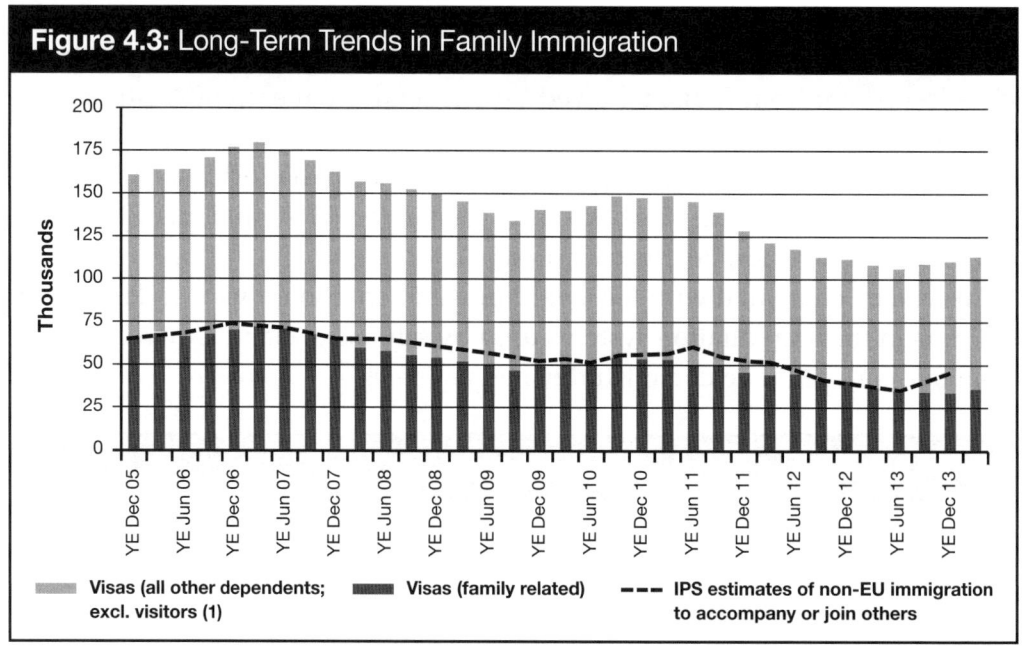

- Visas (all other dependents; excl. visitors (1))
- Visas (family related)
- --- IPS estimates of non-EU immigration to accompany or join others

Source: Home Office, Immigration Statistics January–March 2014 as cited by ONS

Figure 4.4: Long-Term Trends in Grants of Citizenship

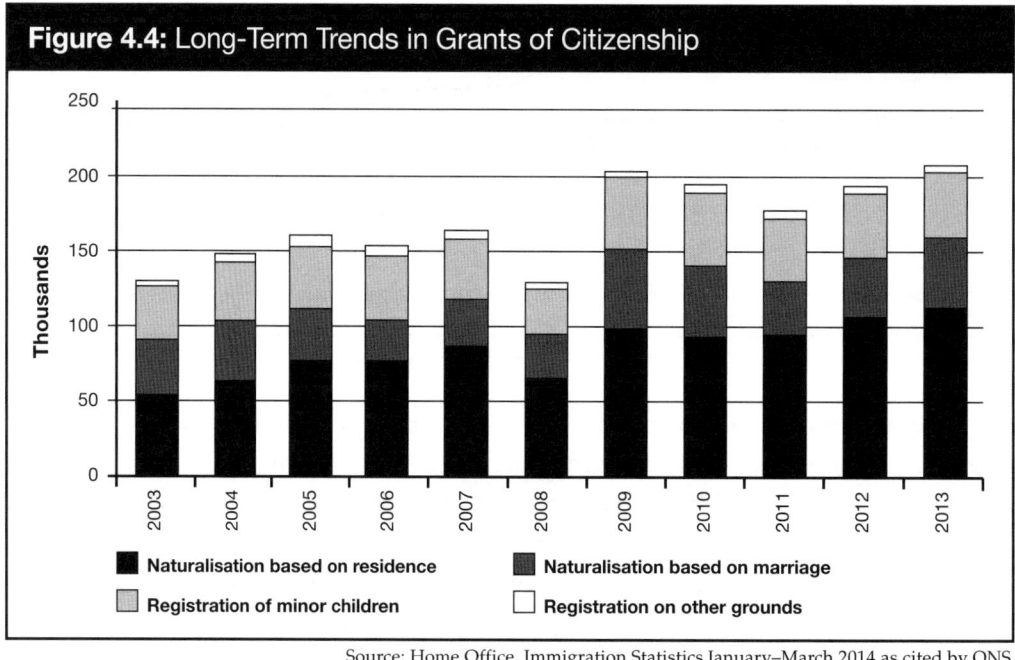

- Naturalisation based on residence
- Naturalisation based on marriage
- Registration of minor children
- Registration on other grounds

Source: Home Office, Immigration Statistics January–March 2014 as cited by ONS

These are overwhelmingly not EU nationals, since EEA citizenship already gives them considerable right of residence in the UK without following the naturalisation path – though interestingly several thousand Poles do feature in the top ten of countries of origin, further confirming that the UK has been lucky in having them as a culturally sympathetic migrant workforce.

These figures reveal that Whitehall has failed to control immigration even amongst those where there is a legal capability to do so. The problem then becomes exacerbated amongst EU/EEA nationals. One of the 'Four Freedoms' associated with the single market is that of the freedom of people's movement. Measures taken to reduce some of the border control gaps cannot be applied to these people. The result is that while 11,000 fewer non-EU citizens immigrated over the last year compared with the 2012 statistic, 43,000 more EU citizens did.

201,000 EU citizens immigrated in the year ending December 2013, up from 158,000 the previous year. 125,000 EU citizens immigrated for work in the year ending December 2013, up from 95,000. 23,000 EU2 (Romanian and Bulgarian) citizens immigrated in the year ending December 2013, up from 9,000 the previous year. The largest increases in National Insurance number registrations in the year ending March 2014 were for citizens of Romania (up 29,000 to 47,000), Poland (up 11,000 to 102,000), Italy (up 9,000 to 42,000) and Bulgaria (up 7,000 to 18,000) from the previous year.[4]

A picture paints a thousand words, so here is that reality transposed into an historical context.

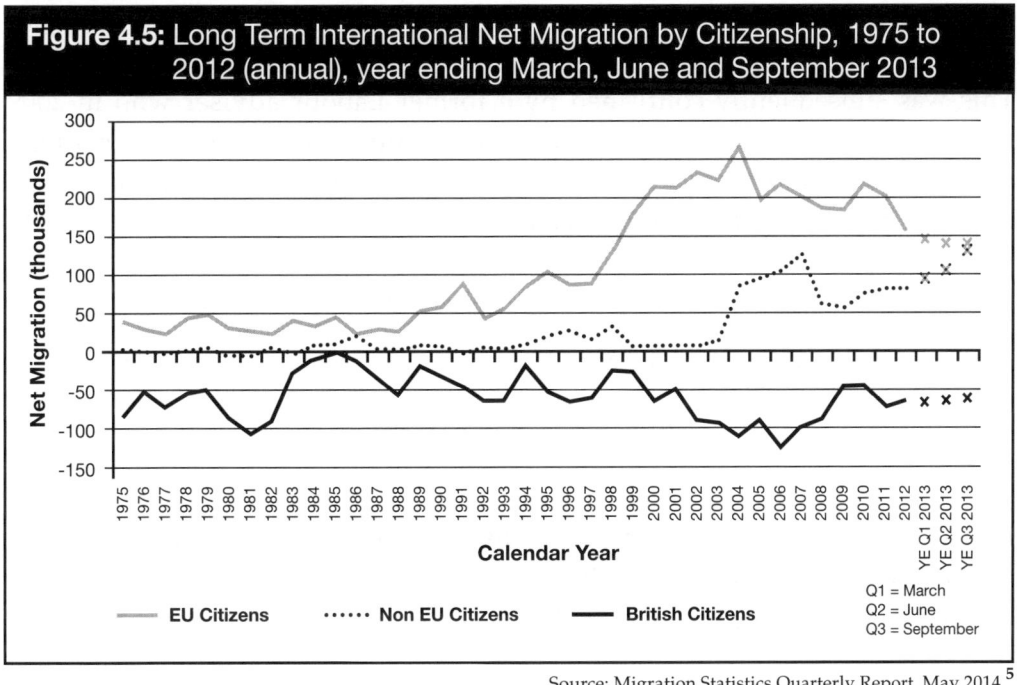

Figure 4.5: Long Term International Net Migration by Citizenship, 1975 to 2012 (annual), year ending March, June and September 2013

Source: Migration Statistics Quarterly Report, May 2014 [5]

To summarise, then, it is clear that any attempt to bring immigration numbers back under control depends on two key factors. The first involves properly addressing the immigration numbers of non-EU nationals. Here, coalition policy has only been a partial success, and merely on one of the two central elements. Only the bogus colleges front has been addressed – and while this has had a striking impact it has not done much more than dent the total numbers. These gains are now being lost behind the reality of large numbers of EU/EEA nationals entering the UK workforce.

Culturally in the meantime, the sum identity issue that makes immigration such a flash point is being exacerbated by the continuing emigration of large numbers of indigenous Brits. Financially meanwhile, these are often asset rich when they leave while the immigrants are often asset poor.

This policy is a critical one to get right and an inevitable one to address. Indeed, in so doing, we are simply recognising the significance that some of our political adversaries cynically attach to it. Those who endorse a level of mega-immigration that exceeds the ability of society to integrate the newcomers are deliberately attempting social change by different means. It is being used not only as a tool of social change but also of political subversion; not always successfully, given that many immigrants themselves believe that present immigration levels are excessive.

The shameless brazen cynicism of it all can best be seen by such documents as that obtained by an FOI request in 2001, clearly identifying the engineering of social change through mass immigration as a Labour government objective. This was subsequently confirmed by a former Labour adviser who in 2009 penned a piece for the Evening Standard admitting that policy over a nine year period was to run a deliberate yet denied policy of mass immigration, contrary incidentally to manifesto commitments, with the intent of overt party political gain.[6]

This seems to be a successful and rare application of Bertold Brecht's lines:

> The people had forfeited the confidence of the government and could win it back only by redoubled efforts. Would it not be easier in that case for the government to dissolve the people and elect another?

In this context, attacks on critics for using the term 'swamping' as inflammatory – just as they motored on towards turning Leicester into a majority non-white city and London itself into a majority non-white British capital – is cant.[7] London's own changed example can be viewed in the table below.[8]

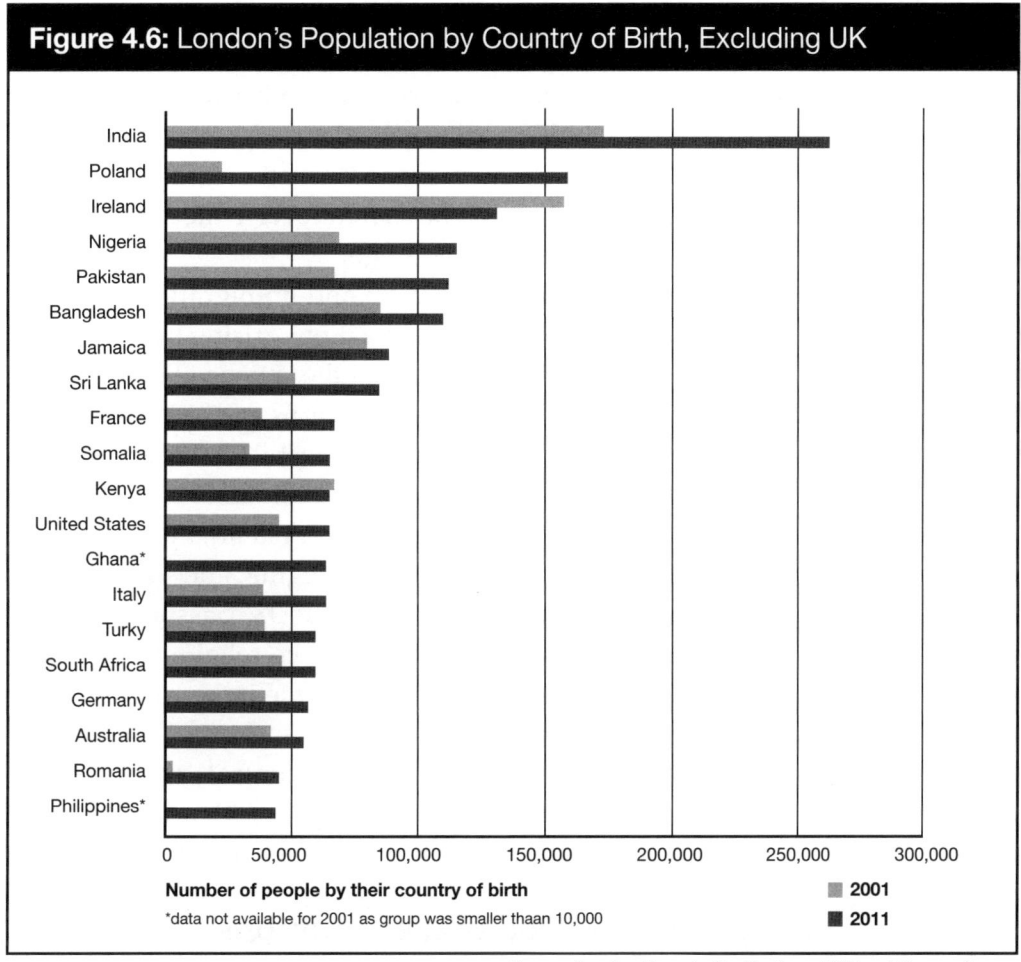

Figure 4.6: London's Population by Country of Birth, Excluding UK

Country	
India	
Poland	
Ireland	
Nigeria	
Pakistan	
Bangladesh	
Jamaica	
Sri Lanka	
France	
Somalia	
Kenya	
United States	
Ghana*	
Italy	
Turky	
South Africa	
Germany	
Australia	
Romania	
Philippines*	

Number of people by their country of birth
*data not available for 2001 as group was smaller thaan 10,000

■ 2001
■ 2011

Source: London Poverty Profile, from ONS and Census figures

Even this image is partial. An issue that also needs to be addressed within any truly coherent immigration plan ('policy' as a term has perhaps lost its credibility) relates to the strategic gain from immigration. This covers the mutual benefits that can be gained from using these communities as springboards to developing world markets, particularly in the Commonwealth. The problem lies in the self-selecting nature of the current immigration prioritisation mechanism, since it is largely associated with family reunification where some members are already within the UK.

A majority of immigrants, particularly from the Indian subcontinent, appear to be drawn from a far from diverse range of communities – Mirpur/Kotla/Bhimber in Pakistan, Sylhet in Bangladesh, and Punjab in India (especially

Jullundur). Whatever the merits of applying this approach in terms of guaranteeing some measure of independent support on arrival, it does mean that immigrants are not being selected primarily on the basis of skill sets or talent, and it does not generate a wide-ranging set of language and cultural ties needed to generate bridges across the entire economy of these nations. As the author of one short study observes, it would be as if in reverse the subcontinent largely accepted emigrants just from Middlesbrough.[9]

This is not a book though about multiculturalism and immigration; certainly not about that part of it which goes beyond the obligations arising from the EU's four freedoms.[10] Yet in assessing the consequences of the actions of government to date, it is important to accept the validity of the concerns and risks associated with such wilful and deceitful mismanagement in the past.[11] Examples of failed cultural overlap include the Rushdie Affair; radical imams who support terrorism (exacerbated by our mismatched human rights system); the non-British practices evident in Tower Hamlets and postal ballot rigging; and the existence of faith- or ethnicity-driven mass demonstrations by UK passport holders lobbying on behalf of a foreign power, national group, or co-religionaries, where the UK has no national interest and particularly where the issues involved are controversial, complex and partisan.

So immigration itself needs to be brought under control, to retain the commonality of British values and halt the development of identity ghettos.[12] Addressing this problem goes far wider than simply trying to fix the EU treaties.

Big problems need bigger solutions

Bottom lines up front

- A joined-up policy response is needed across Whitehall.
- This includes both push and pull factors.
- The government of the day had better be ready for the second order consequences that will follow reduced levels of immigration.
- It's no use blaming immigrants for unemployment when the UK government has been structurally failing to address getting UK nationals into work.
- Immigration can, when managed coherently, be a benefit to the economy where there is a genuine skills shortage.

The response must be joined up across government. It is a mistake to take the control of our borders as a matter in isolation, reliant on issuing an edict to the person in uniform holding the passport stamp. Or for that matter to mistakenly believe either it can be fixed by simply renegotiating the EU treaties, and certainly not by an approach that excludes fundamentally amending them at all. The causes and effects of our high levels of immigration require intelligent, interlocking responses.

It is significant that the Prime Minister has himself now begun to reference this reality. Speaking at the CBI 2014 annual conference, he observed, 'the flip side of the coin on immigration is a welfare system that rewards work and an education system that turns out people with the skills necessary to do the jobs that we're creating in our country today. And no immigration policy will succeed unless it's accompanied by that welfare and that education reform as well.'

Each of three key issues should not be taken in isolation. The first is that of instances of skilled labour shortfall: this is where EU migrants usefully plug a gap, although the domestic workforce should be being trained up to fulfil that role wherever possible.

The second relates to where unskilled EU labour should be filled by unemployed UK citizens 'getting on their bike', essentially where they are disincentivised by our current benefits system. This is our fault as a nation, by allowing migrant workers to fill a gap of our own making, and where we need to motivate an aspirational young workforce that in some cases has lost the habits of graft and the fire for self-improvement. Fixing this problem is not simply about stopping EU workers, but making our own unemployed workers fit and willing to do the job.

The third issue concerns the most outrageous group, be it numerically a minority – benefits claimants from abroad, abusing the relatively weak UK system: this is tiered and non-contributory unlike mechanisms in many other EU countries, and set at a rate that is much higher. Measures put forward to decrease pay outs to cover three months for new arrivals may now partially help, if they are legally secure; but in a context of joined-up responses they will not deter potential workers taking a chance by trying to land a job on arrival and adding additional hands to a finite labour market. As a positive measure, such moves do target a very visible and irksome minority that generates particular hostility against migrants.

The sorts of solutions that are needed must correspondingly reflect these different objectives. If we are to opt to remain within the EEA bandwidth, our treaties need to be amended so that they are ECJ-proof, redirecting the freedom associated with the mass labour force back towards the earlier concept of workers being freed from town hall red tape. Case law will inevitably see attempts to weaken this using the other three freedoms, so the treaties themselves need to be explicit in making countries of origin responsible for paying social security cover to people who have not been in the social security system of a country of residence for less than a trigger threshold (after which, as they are contributing in taxes, it is only fair that they should get a – financially appropriate – level of safeguard). Free movement without benefits should also come with those rights subject to being lifted on the basis of criminality. It should be sufficient for an individual to be awarded prison time, even if suspended, for the right of residency to be revoked. That might also be triggered by two fines at the Magistrates Court. Such an approach would have the added benefit of encouraging foreign workers to take out car insurance, which in some parts of the country has become a significant issue. Residency could further be refused where prison time has been spent in other EU countries, an admission which would have to be set out as part of any residency/National Insurance application requirement.

But more rigid border controls and residency requirements are only part of the joined-up response. Social security reform itself needs to shift to return to the original principles of the Beveridge Report, rather than risk acting as a demotivator and disincentive: a trampoline rather than a mere safety net.

The flip side of this involves giving our school leavers the training to succeed. In part this is about overcoming past grade inflation, so employers can trust the standards implied by UK certificates. It's also about having a school system that teaches the basics of reading, writing and arithmetic competently. That all falls out from reforming the way we teach.

Success here also implies additional emphasis on motivation and aspiration, particularly in terms of encouraging career progression into industry or retail, rather than accepting excessive promotion of the cult of personality (including sports). To this, future generations need to rediscover the tradition of starting at the bottom, building up work experience, and moving on up rather than holding on whilst on benefits for an ideal job. The contrast with migrant workforce attitudes in this regard is anecdotally astonishing. Coupled with this, and already begun, is a willingness to develop vocational training and apprenticeships as valid career paths that afford valid experience, and which are useful to businesses themselves for long-term expansion and recruitment of known and valued staff.

The parallel problem of health tourism should be tackled at the same time. Hospitals need to get tougher on demanding proof of eligibility for NHS provision. In part this is strategic, to clamp down on such abuse and avoid the National Health Service becoming the World Health Service. To achieve this though, we need to start addressing failings in our human rights legal system, and in particular certain pernicious aspects of the Strasbourg coverage. Cases such as *D vs United Kingdom* (1997) have ludicrously set the framework for our courts to be corralled into providing taxpayer-funded healthcare to foreign criminals whose very actions put other people into the NHS in the first place: we need out of the ECHR to correct this.[13] But our hospitals also need to check proof of eligibility and to better chase up repayment from the home service provider via the EHIC (the European Health Insurance Card) and bilateral cross-payments systems. Where eligibility is subsequently found to be wrong, treatment should stop. An 'NHS passport' is worth considering as an associated prop, though sundry IT fiascos teach us to be cautious about relying too heavily on that route. Furthermore, existing EHIC documents have not been routinely asked for. Any demand and use would have to be uniform. But an efficiently run model would save the NHS anywhere between £100 million and £2bn a year.

Then of course there is the matter of benefits reform for overseas nationals. Annex E contrasts the UK's level of benefits with those in other countries, and it's self-evident why some might see it even if not an area for abuse, then as a ready prop set at a level they could quite reasonably live off if having difficulties finding work. As a non-Eurozone country and therefore with a more robust economy, where English is the official language, with established communities originating from across the world, with a comparatively well-paid workforce, and a reputation for providing opportunities for foreign workers (as demonstrated by failing to delay worker access to EU11 nationals on their EU accession), we should not be surprised if such large numbers of people try to enter the UK labour market, and correspondingly why their occasional failure risks associating this country with a significant additional social security bill.

Benefits reform may garner some support from other EU countries, though realistically leaders of countries whose nationals fare well out of our current predicament may be disinclined to support us. Recent changes fought for by the UK are a step forward, but still short of what's required.[14] We need to prepare for unilateral changes, and it should not be beyond our wit to generate a scheme that if challenged in Luxembourg would drag other countries' systems down with us and therefore win their support.[15] We also need to be clear that we are not prepared to go down the bear trap route of generating uniform or common EU benefits systems, which is a well signposted path to further European economic and fiscal integration. This is, however, one area where levelling down by agreeing a common minimum per capita threshold across all benefits might be a way out of our own folly, especially if agreed via a (non-binding) recommendation rather than a directive.

Taken as a whole, what does this all mean? In sum, getting back control of our national immigration policy requires a massive effort across all of government. As Table 4.1 below demonstrates, there are a range of areas where reform is needed in order to address what Dr Richard North correctly identifies as both the 'push' and 'pull' effects and encourage migration to happen in the first place, even without the issue of there being open borders. This table suggests some of the key issues that would need to be addressed internationally as part of any new system. Without fixing these – and the list is only partial and illustrative – we will be merely substituting a lack of border controls with long queues at ports of entry and a surge in illegal entry.[16]

Table 4.1: European-Related Precursors to Gaining Control of the UK's Borders

Issue	Consequence	Response	Dept Lead
Control over entrance	Actual right to control entry at borders.	Remove UK from EEA (i.e. not just EU, owing to four freedoms). Renegotiate EU trade terms in tandem.	Home
Control over deportation	Reduced ability to permanently deport undesirables. Social disorder. Rough sleeper encampments. Untaxed and uninsured drivers.	Suspend application of ECHR (esp Article 8). Enforce enforcement.	Home, PCCs
Zero tolerance of criminal activity	EEA nationals enjoy a greater threshold of prison time before deportation than other foreign nationals.	Over 2011 there were 49,233 Daily Activity File (DAF) updates over an EU national within the England and Wales legal system: notification of a conviction or breach should be a sufficient trigger to allow deportation and barring from re-entry. Requires a database to match. Also needs reduction of legal threshold of deportation trigger to match non-EEA nationals, which should also in turn be dropped to absolute zero-tolerance. You break the law, you get deported.	MoJ

Issue	Consequence	Response	Dept Lead
Foreign nationals in UK prisons	Reduced options to deport convicts to home jails in order to free up space. As at 30 June 2014, 10,834 out of 85,509 inmates were foreign nationals.	Start to draft bilaterals with countries of origin: first officially identify what those countries are!	MoJ
Management of borders	Planning to continue to allow workers in where the economy needs them.	Canadian etc points system, with points-per-job revisited every year. Lower numbers actually awarded with greater emphasis on short-term stay. Actually assess what skill sets are needed but based on industry input not Whitehall central planning.	Employment
Illegal entry	Stowaways and Sangatte.	Further develop the 'forward frontier' principle. Do not encourage additional illegal migration by spending more on search and rescue in the Mediterranean but run PR campaigns in home countries to deter based on risks, and a proven policy of deportation without financial gain. Liaison with local law enforcement to help them catch human traffickers and sequester proceeds of crime locally.	Home, FCO
Early access to welfare	Safety net for economic migrants to 'chance it' without prior work arrangements; some celebrated cases of social security abuse.	Welfare access by foreign nationals entirely dependent on bilaterals and what access and rates are available to UK nationals on their country of origin. Minimum pay in lead time by foreign nationals. Availability only to those arriving with contract containing notification period. Remove access to skills training by migrant workers.	Social Security
Grandfather rights	Existing EEA residency rights would be legally deemed to carry across.	Legal clarification that any changes in the law do not mean current foreign workers retain blanket right to stay under old provisions.	Home
Remove ambiguity over future expat residency rights.	Possible confusion over UK expats' rights overseas, particularly Spain and to a lesser extent France, plus ROI. (In fact North America and Australasia are bigger expat locations for UK nationals.) Presently, OAPs may retire abroad if they have secure income plus comprehensive health insurance, so this is largely an administrative issue only.	Issue is overwhelmingly confined to these three countries. ROI arrangements are long standing; French have a major expat community in London; Brits in Spain largely retired (not taking jobs but paying local services from a pension and holding health insurance) or are supporting the tourist trade, and therefore no economic drain to the host. There is correspondingly merely a need to clarify with these governments that bilaterals are sought, possibly allowing for variably privileged access in return.	Social Security

Issue	Consequence	Response	Dept Lead
Anglosphere access	Increase access rights to UK by nations which share the Queen as our common Head of State; accelerated access to investors and wealth multipliers (e.g. leading academics) across wider Commonwealth.	Bilaterals to streamline visa access. Physically changing the 'EEA' queue in passport control. Analysis of changes that may be required to e-passport and other international agreements involving these countries.	FCO

But these changes in themselves largely provide opportunity. They do not of themselves generate the full framework structurally needed both to make the system work and for the public to regain trust. Restoring sovereign control over the nation's borders is not the solution itself. So in addition to these reforms which directly affect the EU, the next Prime Minister is recommended to carry out a number of complementary domestic changes – and these are set out in Table 4.2 below.

Table 4.2: Further Reforms That Would Then Follow

Issue	Consequence	Response	Dept Lead
Weakly enforced overstay rules	Encourages breaking rules.	More enforcement staff; greater fines for breaches; breaches generate stiff no-readmittance black marks; review of IT cross-compliance by departments.	Home
Nine million National Insurance (NI) numbers estimated issued to foreign nationals	Uncertainty over fraud.	Publish NI details in these cases online (not UK nationals as home NI can be used as an identity check). Stronger system allows for use of NI as part of any migration management scheme. Tighten up resultant rights from trivial NI pay-in e.g. by selling Big Issue (as per the Firuṭa Vasile Housing Benefit eligibility case).	DWP
Backlog	The default setting will be to allow residency applicants to stay owing to delays in processing their claims (regardless of actual merits).	The default setting should be the burden of proof is on the claimant. Ban claims from (regularly reviewed) White List of countries. Limit appeals options and to be held within 7 days of first hearing.	Home
Passport rights	Inability to deport joint passport holders with family ties, or first generation UK nationals.	Revisit legal obligations of UK to passport holders and those who have destroyed papers (statelessness issues). Explore development of a Manus Island/Lampedusa facility to dissuade illegal economic migrants pretending to be asylum seekers.	Home

Issue	Consequence	Response	Dept Lead
Bogus marriages	Back door right to stay.	Greater priority in prosecuting. Seize assets. Encourage churches to defrock those found guilty (placing at risk their charitable tax status).	MoJ
Excessive language rights	Additional costs to Police Forces and legal service obliged to provide support in foreign languages. Discourages integration.	Increased use of remote services (phone interpreters and static provision legally sufficient to caution by handing a prepared translated card) for routine aspects of cases. Possible pooling of PCC language provision.	Home, MoJ, PCC
Health tourism	Financial loss to Treasury.	NHS to enforce reclaims from home country, revisit bilaterals, requirement of visitor health insurance, no subsidised medication at point of distribution without state reciprocation. Similar principles for dental care. However, adapt new policies to minimise risks of transmittable diseases e.g. TB.	Health
Lack of UK nationals in workforce to replace foreign workers	Job gaps on introduction of border changes; wage inflation; loss of UK competitiveness.	Encourage UK workers to take up these jobs by cutting welfare if refused.	Social Security
Untrained UK nationals to replace foreign workers	Unmotivated and ill-equipped workforce to take the place of migrant workers.	A central issue without which immigration changes would leave a policy chasm. Greater emphasis from job advisors at schools on low paid stepping stone work; massive improvements in schooling system and delivery of 'Three Rs'; deflation in school grading; continued expansion of vocational training.	Education
Wage abuse by gangmasters	Foreign workers paid less than minimum wage; undercuts employment of UK nationals.	Prioritised enforcement of existing laws on minimum wages, and criminal prosecution. Also: helpline/ support for abused foreign workers to assist in return home, to break power of end-point abuse.	Treasury (wages transparency)
Housing abuse by gangmasters	Multiple residency in excess of maximum occupancy in rented accommodation, as part of undercutting wages paid to UK nationals.	Enforcement of occupancy laws. Possible change of law to permit sequestration of assets so used.	Local councils
Danger of overregulation under existing system	Gangmasters Licensing Authority (GLA) risks adding red tape costs to agricultural producers (farms and forestry).	Abolish GLA/licensing to reduce red tape costs to agriculture and replace with direct law enforcement and reliance on an expanded helpline system.	Home

Issue	Consequence	Response	Dept Lead
Family rights	Residency rights extended to large families not just to one individual. Reduction of ethnic diversity amongst immigrant communities, resulting in weaker trade opportunities by these groups acting as an economic bridge to their country of origin. Employers bring in family rather than employ existing UK nationals.	Individuals to apply separately and solely on their own merits (also ECHR relevant).	Home
Language use	Failure of immigrant to integrate on arrival. Additional costs for the delivery of services.	Increased emphasis as part of points system; increased requirement for immigrants to be conversant in English in order to be better aware of the broader community and environment. DCLG to dissuade multilingual (exc. Welsh, Gaelic) literature by councils. Councils to focus on English language courses for existing first generation immigrants with poor English.	FCO consulates, DCLG
Increased house prices	Increased population increases strain on housing stock, therefore on house prices; yet also demands higher social or subsidised housing owing to native unemployed and immigrants on low pay.	Reduction of dependence on foreign workforce will reduce house prices; government will need to reappraise its attitudes and perceptions (media messaging) towards a fall in house prices, along with the associated potential for negative equity. This is not, however, justification for further state intervention on top of existing ill-considered schemes. Long term a reduction in such prices is a national gain but Whitehall is endorsing a massive bubble.	Treasury
Ambulance-chasing lawyers	Imbeds delay into the system, adds cost, discourages deportations, and rewards bad lawyers when many others actually get a bad deal.	Legal clarity on limits to appeals for deportation. Finite pay outs per legal firm and a disincentive nominal baseline payment to be paid on any appeal that legal aid does not cover. Australian system of media advertising legal firms (dispassionate and basic contact details).	Justice
Mismanaged asylum policy in tandem	Asylum seekers go off radar, or remain an underused asset in certain cases.	Better management of asylum seekers cases: legal requirement for them to keep location notified or else case defaults. Asylum seekers with specific skill sets (e.g. a surgeon, linguist) may be authorised to undertake community work where skills are of value, in order to reduce state subsidy required. Utterly dismiss any prospect of amnesty for illegal asylum seekers, which encourages the practice.	Home

Issue	Consequence	Response	Dept Lead
Prioritising the integrators	A more integrated society with a reduction in extremism.	Increased focus on this aspect (e.g. passports for Gurkhas, greater emphasis on access by nationals who have the Queen as head of state) or come from an environment with established 'British' principles (whose definition might be debated) and are therefore capable of ready social integration. Be prepared to argue that an interest in getting a UK passport is not the same as being in the national interest to giving them one.	Home

5

Money Still Matters

Financial services[1]

> **Bottom lines up front**
> - The City's welfare is of massive importance to the UK, and it is under EU threat.

The City is of critical importance to the UK economy. Compared with other European economies, it features disproportionately as a national asset and opportunity, as well as risk. This means for instance that the failure of the single market to properly liberalise services has had a worse impact upon the UK compared with other countries, and why the lure (perhaps an enduring false prospect) has long bedazzled the FCO in assessing the long-term advantages of remaining an integral part of the single market club.

Table 5.1 sets out the extent to which this is so. London is the EU's largest financial centre such that it is sometimes referred to as the 'EU's financial capital'. London is significantly ahead of France and Germany in all specified areas except exchange-traded derivatives.

Table 5.1: Financial Markets Share by Country as a percentage

	UK	US	Japan	France	Germany	Sing'e	HK	Others
Cross-border bank lending (end-2012)	18	11	11	8	8	3	3	38
Foreign exchange turnover (April 2013)	41	19	6	3	2	6	4	19
Exchange-traded derivatives, number of contracts traded (2012)	7	34	2	-	8	-	1	48

	UK	US	Japan	France	Germany	Sing'e	HK	Others
Interest rates OTC derivatives turnover (Apr 2013)	49	23	2	7	4	1	1	13
Marine insurance net premium income (2011)	21	6	9	4	4	1	1	54
Fund management (as a source of funds, end-2012)	8	45	7	3	2	-	1	34
Hedge funds assets (end-2012)	18	65	2	1	-	1	1	12
Private equity: investment value (2012)	10	48	1	5	2	1	-	33
Securitisation: issuance (2011)	6	73	2	1	1	-	-	17

Source: *TheCityUK*, 'Key facts about the UK as an international financial centre', October 2013

Table 5.2, below, meanwhile sets out the UK share of the EU's financial markets

Table 5.2: UK Share of Financial Markets in the EU or in Europe

	per cent share	Date of information
Interest rate OTC derivatives trading (EU)	74	Apr-2013
Foreign exchange trading (EU)	78	Apr-2013
Hedge fund assets (Europe)	85	2012
Private equity funds raised (Europe)	57	2012
Marine insurance premiums (EU)	54	2012
Fund management (EU)	50	2012
Financial services GDP (EU)	37	2012
Equity market capitalisation (LSE)	24	2012
Bank lending (EU)	18	2012
Banks assets (Europe)	26	2012/13
Insurance premiums (EU)	22	2012
Financial and professional services employment (EU)	19	2012

Source: *TheCityUK*, 'UK & the EU: a mutually beneficial relationship', December 2013

Moreover, TheCityUK's research concludes[2]:
- The UK provides more than 40 per cent of all City-type financial services activity in the EU and is the leading European centre for investment and private banking, hedge funds, private equity, exchange traded derivatives and sovereign wealth funds;

- The UK has a leading share of trading in interest rate over the counter (OTC) derivatives (74 per cent of EU total), foreign exchange turnover (78 per cent), management of hedge funds assets (85 per cent) and private equity funds (57 per cent), international insurance premiums (54 per cent) and fund management assets (50 per cent);
- Twice as many euros are traded in the UK than all other EU member states combined. London is therefore the 'trading centre for the Eurozone';
- 164 financial services firms from the rest of the EU are based in the UK. And EU banks in the UK hold £1.4tn assets – 17 per cent of total UK bank assets;
- The UK is also a leading provider of related professional services and is the biggest centre for international legal services and dispute resolution, accounting, management consulting, and financial and professional services education and training. All of the ten largest EU headquartered law firms are located in London.

The City contributes a trade surplus in the order of £60bn annually; a ballpark £130bn or around a tenth of GDP: more than double France and Germany combined as a share of their GDPs. This makes this sector a critically important one for the Chancellor and Foreign Secretary to get right.

London has a wide range of advantages over its Eurozone competitors. These include the availability of skilled personnel (reminding us of the need to have a tailored rather than a blanket immigration/work policy); a comparatively benign regulatory environment; access to international financial markets; the existence of business infrastructure; access to customers; a fair and just business environment; a business-friendly government; the rule of law; non-punitive corporate and personal tax regimes; acceptable operational costs; access to suppliers of professional services; availability of commercial property (albeit at very high prices); plus cultural issues relating to quality of life, and also the primary use of the English language. Reviewing that list, most are subject to variables that depend on Brussels, and are increasingly subject to attempts to intervene there (a point to which we shall later return across the UK economy).

One problem that therefore emerges is that London is under enduring threat of being hobbled by its direct competitors, by bureaucratising meddling, or by excessive regulation intended to curb excess but which carries disproportionate incidental costs. In some cases, it transpires it's all three, and that the EU is a problem multiplier.

The case histories of such issues as artists' resale rights, van regulations, or outboard motor specifications demonstrate that regulations can and do get wilfully used to target foreign competition, typically with the end result of driving business not *across* the EU but *out of it altogether* to third countries that avoid needless costs and burdens.[3] One 'win' for the UK was the Commission's decision to scrap their plans to grant ESMA sole and direct supervision of Libor,[4] Euribor and other benchmarks in September 2013, though we can predict the issue will be revisited in the future. Other damaging examples have included the European Systemic Risk Board (European Banking Authority), the Directive on Alternative Investment Fund Managers, Solvency II and minimum assets requirements, the Capital Requirements Directive, and even the attempt to push a requirement for euro clearing houses to be within the Eurozone. In this latter case, the UK has even taken Frankfurt to the ECJ for the first time. Paris has long had its eye on monopolising Eurozone activity, as confirmed in a leaked confidential Banque de France report that recommended measures to abrogate to itself from London the management of credit default swaps. With Solvency II, the Chief Executive of Legal and General, Nigel Wilson, in August 2014 revealed that it had meant his company wasting £150m of the £170m it had been forced to spend as a result.

A particularly serious development for the City was the ECJ's rejection of the UK's attempt to block the Financial Transaction Tax (FTT). The UK is not planning to introduce the FTT (11 member states are), but the measure has extraterritorial effect. If a deal is done in London involving assets that are covered by the charge, the tax will have to be collected here. The ruling underlines the limits of the UK's influence to contain Eurozone-based initiatives taken forward under 'enhanced cooperation' that may affect the City, certainly as concerns the early stages of Brussels negotiations and before political favours are expended. The FTT case turned on a relatively new EU procedure, which allows a subset of countries to continue with a reform if EU-wide agreement is impossible, as long as the initiative does not 'damage' the single market. It is a path allowing for significant Eurozone integration in future.

Pre-empting long-term decline

Bottom lines up front

- The threat to the City from the EU will increase over time, even as an EU member – and even worse as a Eurozone member.
- A firewall is needed, and because of existing pan-EU structures that can be best generated through a new treaty.

Trade in financial services is therefore clearly of importance to the British economy. Trade with the EU is too. But, apart from our concerns over possible changes to the regulatory and trading regime within the EU, we would caveat all analysis of UK-EU trade with the knowledge that the EU is a relatively shrinking part of the world economy – and this includes, critically, the financial markets. The Fresh Start project reported:

> Whilst in 2005 the UK, Germany, France, Spain and Italy accounted for 27% of global banking assets, PriceWaterhouseCoopers projects that in 2050 that will have decreased to 12.5%. PwC also projects that the BRIC countries will see their share leap from the 2005 figure of 7.9% to 32.9% in 2050.[5]

Such major changes will inevitably have implications for future prospects for UK trade. Meanwhile, two inter-related and probably irreversible developments in the EU also have significant implications for financial services. They will inevitably affect London's competitiveness globally and regionally.

The first is the considerable increase in financial services regulation since 2008, the year of the financial crisis and the ensuing recession. There is little doubt that many within the EU have taken the opportunity, rightly or wrongly, to step up controls over the financial markets in the belief that liberalised 'Anglo-Saxon' markets were responsible, at least in part, for the severity of the recession. For example, German Finance Minister Wolfgang Schäuble said in October 2011:

> We have to fight the causes of this crisis, and the main reasons of the crisis are a lack of financial market regulation and an abundance of Government deficits and debt.[6]

French President Nicolas Sarkozy, not a noted left winger, welcomed the appointment of his countryman Michel Barnier as EU Commissioner for the Internal Market and Financial Services in 2010 as a 'defeat for Anglo-Saxon capitalism'. As a consequence there has been an abundance of new rules and restrictions. As Fresh Start noted:

> Increased EU regulation is threatening to constrict the activity of our financial services industry – a staggering 49 regulations, many aimed at restricting financial services activity, have been proposed since 2008.

The second development concerns the establishment of the EU Banking Union, in which the ECB will be the supervisor for the large Eurozone banks. Non-euro countries may join the Banking Union if they wish and many probably will. The risks for the UK are, firstly, that it will gradually lose influence to the Eurozone countries in the European Banking Authority (EBA) and, secondly, that the EBA will gradually lose influence to the ever-more powerful ECB.

At the UK's behest a 'double majority lock' for EBA decision making was agreed in December 2012.[7] The procedure is intended to ensure that the UK will not be outvoted by the Eurozone and allies, acting as a caucus, under the current QMV rules operating in the EBA – the Eurozone currently has nearly 62 per cent of the required 74 per cent to pass decisions under QMV. So, in addition to QMV, it was agreed that there must also be a simple majority of 'Single Supervisory Mechanism (SSM) Participants' (i.e. Eurozone banks monitors) and a simple majority of the 'SSM non-participants', in order to guarantee the influence of the 'outs' including Britain. However there will be a review of these voting arrangements if/when the number of non-participants falls to four. The odds must be heavily stacked against the 'double majority' vote surviving such a review. Moreover, with the delayed post-Lisbon changes to QMV procedures finally being introduced, the Eurozone countries, acting as a caucus, automatically outvote the non-Eurozone countries.

Correspondingly, to return to the analysis of Fresh Start:

> With impending banking union, there is a real risk that Eurozone countries will begin to act as a bloc; outvoting the UK on key financial issues.

And the House of Lords has recently stated:

> As the Eurozone moves towards closer integration the UK will need to work hard to influence the debate, which it needs to do for its own good, for the good of the City of London, and the good of all 28 members of the EU.[8]

On a closely related point, with the UK outside the Eurozone, there are clear pressures to transfer much of London's euro-business to financial centres within the Eurozone. Christian Noyer, Governor of the Bank of France, said in December 2012:

> We're not against some business being done in London but the bulk of the [euro] business should be under our control. That's the consequence of the choice by the UK to remain outside the euro area.

Reflecting on the twin challenges of increased regulation and the implications of Banking Union, John Gapper, writing in the FT, suggested that the UK's strategic choice going forward was 'poor'. It can either remain in the EU 'fending off Eurozone-driven rules the best it can' or 'the City supports Brexit, losing the European role and turning into a free-floating global hub'. He concluded, 'The City is on the cusp of history again'.[9]

So to summarise, increased EU regulation is threatening to constrict a vital national interest, our financial services industry. Over the period 2008-2012, an average of a damaging regulation a month was being churned out by the Commission. No wonder that Fresh Start concluded that up to the financial crisis the single market in financial services had been genuinely liberalising and helpful, but that was no longer the case.

Given the undoubted importance of the City to the UK economy, this is disquieting. The UK is in this area as in many others being forced to choose between accepting disproportionately damaging regulatory burdens, or redefining its access to the single market and the customs union. In the City's case, the prognosis is particularly bleak as the ultimate choice on present terms of EU association involves either Eurozone assimilation (with all the economic disasters that such entails) or meekly accepting being slowly choked. The hundred dollar question for the City is, therefore, what is the difference between (i) being in the EU, outside the Eurozone and (ii) being outside the EU. This is the small print the negotiators will have to define.

The direction is already very clear. The establishment of the ECB's Open Market Transactions (OMT) for 'unlimited' bond-buying by the ECB in September 2012 was accompanied by a statement by its President Mario Draghi, who said that 'within our mandate, the ECB is ready to do whatever it takes to preserve the euro […] Believe me, it will be enough'. The German Constitutional Court challenged the legality of this, but in such matters the ECJ is the EU's arbiter. Then there is the example of the fledgling European Stability Mechanism, a half-trillion bailout system in which the UK was entangled by misuse of an unconnected disaster clause designed for dealing with actual rather than metaphorical earthquakes. The current treaties are no sure guarantor of the City's interests where a Eurozone Crisis demands political action.[10]

If the Eurozone is to survive, there will inevitably be increasing integration. There will be growing concentration of power and decision making in the Eurozone, likely driven by crisis and therefore less inclined to brook compromise and deal in thoughtful measured settlements. Meanwhile, Eurozone institutions, not least of all the ECB, will become ever-more powerful to the detriment of the EU28 institutions. The EBA (European Banking Union) will struggle to retain its influence. The 'outs' (a disparate group in any case) will become ever more peripheral. And for the one 'out' which is determined to remain 'out' (i.e. the UK) our role will be especially peripheral. We'll be in an increasingly isolated position, which can only place our membership in an increasingly compromised position.

All these factors point to the need for the UK to seek a much more modern relationship with the EU, based on trade, but outside the political union. The City can only be protected by a formal firewall, excluding it from the treaties entirely, generated by a new form of treaty association with the Eurozone bloc.

The rebate

> **Bottom lines up front**
>
> - The EU budget is being run on promissory notes.
> - Despite the UK now supposedly being exempt from bailing out Eurozone countries, it is paying out vast sums via main budget back door subsidies.
> - The UK fares badly as a fee-paying member of the EU club.

The huge controversy of the £1.7bn surcharge, and the utter confusion (perhaps deliberate) over whether the UK rebate applied to it, is merely the latest in a string of unsatisfactory episodes relating to British club fees.

One of the enduring and obvious mismatches in the UK's terms of adherence to the EU has been, from the very outset, the forced bribe that constitutes the membership fee. Picking this as an item that needs fixing is simultaneously correct, partial, and impossible.

It's correct, as the UK clearly has long paid in more than its fair share given the relative sizes of the European economies. It's partial, as focusing purely on this issue neglects the far broader economic imbalances associated with EU membership terms, including the hidden costs. It's also impossible given that amending the bill requires the agreement of other member states, and the recipients will demand literally a *quid pro quo* in return for removing themselves from our taxpayers' dole. Any gains made here will be made by surrenders and costs elsewhere.

This suggests only a clean break will fix this enduring deficit and the establishment of a 'lighter' treaty of association short of the full menu. But let's begin with the history.

The arrangement was struck during the initial accession negotiations: we can cynically but accurately attribute its introduction to Brussels negotiators being acutely aware of how desperate their counterparts in the Heath government were to get a deal.

The EU budget has always been funded in three ways. These have been by custom duties and agricultural levies on imports from outside the EEC; a share of VAT revenue; and a share based on Gross National Income. This latter is today the most important, comprising about six tenths of all revenue. World trade agreements have meanwhile cut external tariffs, meaning that these now only constitute one fifth of the revenue. In itself this should remind us of the changing nature of world trade and the obstacles to it that drove us into the EEC in the first place.

The UK has always and obviously been hardest hit because of the nature of its economy. As a world trader and as a major food importer, tariffs proved particularly burdensome. Meanwhile, a central plank of Community spending, the CAP, was less of a gain to the UK given the relative strength and small size of the agricultural economy. Regional aid was backed by London as a means to gain extra money back, but that has since been overtaken by accession from poorer countries better placed to argue for the hand outs on their founding terms.[11] Thus the only occasion the UK came close to being a net beneficiary of Community spending happened, coincidentally, to be at the time of the referendum.[12]

Notably, it was only the very real threat (in breach of treaty obligations, one might add) of withholding the UK budgetary contributions that resulted in the Fontainebleau Rebate agreement. The draft bill to authorise the withholding of the money was even printed – and the fact made known. That of course was not the end of the matter, and the existence of the UK rebate repeatedly appears on the negotiating table, requiring the UK to defensively expend capital trying to retain it. (A simple sleepwalker's veto reflex should suffice [i.e. it should come automatically and without thought, and be expected to be delivered as such], but the FCO is less Parisian than it should be on the matter.[13])

Since that handbagging, the UK government has fallen on the back foot. Under Blair it surrendered the rebate to the newly acceding countries, supposedly because they were too poor to pay it back, though they were already large net recipients of the UK dole. The connected promise to revisit Common Agricultural Policy (CAP) funding in due course proved to be an empty pledge: we can only speculate this far ahead of the release to Kew of the public records whether this was a cynical policy retreat or shallow posturing.

What is clear however is that we can expect more of the same over the coming five years. The press release from the General Affairs Council in June 2005, for example, has a certain Jean-Claude Juncker criticising those who had blocked increases in the finances over what he judged to be minimalist differences, undertaken by some delegations that 'did not have the political will to succeed'.[14] Those eager to review the tea leaves of what the coming EU Commission will be pursuing need only review how the new Commission President acted and spoke while in the driving seat at the Council of Ministers.[15] That list starts with the Luxembourger being the proponent of a freeze in the UK rebate.

Today though, we are confronted with an eroded rebate that is 40 per cent lower than it would have been without the Blair giveaway. Annex F explores what that has meant, but in practical terms it now falls in the area of £3bn lost annually. In 2012–2013, that meant gross payments to the EU of £17.2bn, a rebate of £3.3bn and grants back of £5.2bn. That left a net contribution of £8.6bn – assuming we take the financial worth of the grants back at face value (as opposed to them being non-optimal state subsidies).

Even then, that figure excludes a non-declared additional sum running at 25 per cent of Traditional Own Resources Payments that the government keeps 'to cover the costs of administering collection on behalf of the EU'.[16] This is a key cost that is typically overlooked by those calculating costs of EU membership, and relates to collecting the revenue associated with Sugar Levies (now a remnant) and Customs Duties (which have risen to more than compensate). It currently runs at around £0.75 bn annually – though this figure excludes the burdens of managing VAT receipts and only covers the tax administration of a *tenth* of the revenue assigned to Brussels.

The actual end administration cost of collecting the other UK tithes to Brussels is a matter of open conjecture, including the administration costs required of and passed on to business. Because of relative administration costs, government is encouraged to set it at elevated rates. The nature of this consumption tax is such that it impacts disproportionately on the cost of living for poor families; the form of the tax meanwhile is such that exemptions once disapplied cannot be reintroduced owing to harmonisation obligations.

Notwithstanding that knowledge gap over the main part of the EU tax levy, what we do know is that the TOR 25 per cent is an enduring burden. Over the period 2007–2013, that figure has risen from £605m in admin write-off to £764m in 2013. This makes for a total over seven years of £4,884 million in costs.

In the event, overall this makes for;

- A gross total UK cost in 2012–2013 of significantly over £18bn;
- A gross budgetary handover of £17.2bn;
- A rebate of £3.3bn (which would, without Blair, have been twice this[17]);
- Grants back of £5.2bn;

- These total costs that year of £18bn in return for £8.5bn – or net costs of £9.5bn;
- This excludes any red tape costs, secondary impact of policies (such as the Common Fisheries Policy (CFP) affecting port economies), or loss of competitive advantage (such as to German hauliers, who are closer, gaining better access to Eastern European businesses via improved road networks subsidised by UK taxpayers).

Subsequently, the UK has been bounced with a hike in our expected payments in the order of €2.1bn. Worse, this unexpected bar tab is predicated upon twin insults – firstly, that the ONS and the Treasury have reviewed how they measure the economy in order to be more efficient; and secondly, the economies of Eurozone countries that will benefit from our largesse have taken a battering because of Eurozone membership, a self-inflicted folly which the UK taxpayer is again expected by second order effects to subsidise.

What we can say therefore is that as a country we are being subjected to a fiscal mockery. It is true that some other countries have their own grievances. *Per capita*, Austria, Sweden and the Netherlands also pay a disproportionate share, while Germany is the highest individual contributor. However, the Dutch and Swedes get lump sum rebates, and all four get reduced VAT contributions. So even our existing UK caveat is not that extraordinary.

Based on 2011 figures (the best the Treasury was able to supply for its November 2013 report), sixteen countries were net recipients of EU funding, including Luxembourg and with Spain in fifth place ahead of Belgium and Romania. Six more are marginal payers. Of the remainder, only Sweden, Italy and the UK are not so heavily dependent on single market exports to make a fuss, and of these Italy is politically quiescent owing to its Eurozone exposure (as the dethronement of Berlusconi demonstrated).

So rebate reform is not realistic, unless all political chips are cashed to achieve it – which is essentially what happened at Fontainebleau.

A forced hand

Bottom lines up front
- The EU budget is being run on promissory notes.

> - Despite the UK now supposedly being exempt from bailing out Eurozone countries, it is paying out vast sums via main budget back door subsidies.
> - The UK fares badly as a fee-paying member of the EU club.

Yet despite these negotiating impossibilities, there is a critical need to get financial reform. On the issue simply of public spending, taxpayer money is too often misdirected, wasted, or defrauded. A simple glance at any document on the Court of Auditors website, and in particular the typical nonchalance offered by the Commission in its official responses, reveals that transparency and accountability is spectacularly and enduringly lacking. This may largely be unavoidable, in that there is no sense of ownership and hence of responsibility for spending other people's money that accompanies these grants.

This can only get worse over time. The EU (largely but not exclusively thanks to the European Parliament) has attempted to circumvent limits on its budget by inventive offsetting. It distinguishes between its actual budget and the money it would like to spend by running a commitments deficit, generating a spending backlog and therefore a debt that it expects the Council of Ministers to pay off by increasing the budget every six years to match. The difference between commitments and payments runs at around 5 per cent, consistently exceeding the amount that might reasonably be set aside supposedly in order for sums to be switched from projects that get cancelled. Surplus payments fall into the RAL category, of *Reste à Liquider*. 'RAL refers to all outstanding commitments that remain unpaid at a given point in time. The level of RAL at the end of 2011 (EUR 207 billion) was about EUR 50 billion above the level foreseen when the 2007–2013 financial framework was drawn up. Sixty-five percent of RAL relates to cohesion policy.'[18] To use the euphemism of the MEPs who reviewed the practice, 'They stem directly from the existence of multiannual programmes and the dissociation between commitment and payment appropriations.'[19] When the 2007–2013 budget was being calculated, the organisers catered for an end RAL standing at €180bn. By the end of 2011 it had reached €207bn, and was already being projected to rise to €248bn by 2013.

Significantly, two thirds of this goes on social cohesion spending, covering regional spending and also employment and social spending. These are two areas where the UK historically does badly, in the first instance as it tends to engage far less in major cross-border infrastructure projects (it has the North Sea in the way), but also because it has fewer impoverished regions, and additionally because the Treasury is historically not happy directing money towards dirigiste schemes of unqualified economic viability. UK receipts for 2013 put it in eighth place, behind Belgium and Greece, at levels two fifths of Poland, and half that of Italy, France, Spain and Germany. Yet this area, as well as showing the poor share of UK receipts in key grant areas, is precisely where so much UK-liable RAL Liabilities currently lie.[20]

It will also help for ministers to understand precisely how budget negotiations are made. An excellent example of this relates to the discussions around the EU's six year financial plan for 2014–2020. The participants will recall how the initial maths arising from the agreement appeared to suggest a drop in total and promissory payments for the UK, which turned out to be an actual rise of €1.2bn once the deal progressed and the accounting became clear. Of further interest to us, however, is the manner in which a hidden Eurozone subsidy came to be levied.

Under the terms of the financial agreement reached, EU funding streams were directly tapped for countries whose economies were feeling the Eurozone pinch. It meant an additional €1.4bn for Greece, €1bn for Portugal, €100m for Ireland, €1.8bn for Spain, €1.5bn for Italy, and with outer zone Eurozone countries and territories add another €600m. That made for €6.4bn of invisible subsidy coming from the main EU budget, targeting economies whose sole problem was use of the single currency. The UK, of course, got none of this.

Additionally, €6.0bn would go in total on youth training. However, the trigger was that youth unemployment must be over 25 per cent, meaning that this was effectively another largely Eurozone support. Berlin received another €710m as compensation for still being in East Germany.

Some Eurozone countries were wealthier than others in relative terms, so a safety net was created of 55 per cent of past funding for countries that have gotten wealthier enough to be uprated in relative poverty gradings. Cohesion funding would be opened up again in 2016 so even these restraints could not be guaranteed.

CAP reform does feature. But caveats were added that restricted CAP reform if a state considers the area to have high added value or where change could be disproportionately felt. This provided Paris with large get-out clauses. Meanwhile, grain barons would only see their EU grants capped if their government wanted to see it happen. The UK was notably not one of eleven, mainly Western European, countries named as getting extra cash to support any changes to rural development. France got €1bn, Italy €1.5bn, and even Ireland got €100m.

€23.2bn was targeted at transport projects, an area as we have seen where the UK gains less in grants. To cover all this, the EU's admin budget was raised (despite specific Downing Street attacks) from €8.2bn to €9.4bn to cope.

The UK interest across this is small, compared with the gains to Eurozone countries. But most telling of all is an intriguing rider that allowed for Cohesion Funds to be reduced if governments don't get their deficits in order. The link between pork barrel funding and Germany's subsidies and interests at least couldn't be made clearer.

So we can draw from this a series of conclusions relating to our rather expensive club fees.

Firstly, having a Eurozone opt-out is no protection against subsidising Eurozone economies via the main EU budget. Indeed, with individual countries liable to keep getting into bailout territory, the pressure on the EU budget will only increase. These payments are not firewalled, resulting in massive liabilities to the UK as a major budgetary contributor. Nor are we optimistic about obtaining such a firewall; even getting a fixed liabilities limit for each country will likely only provide a shoji screen in the event of any crisis, as the abuse of the disaster clause (Art 222 TFEU) has already proven. So long as the UK is a significant contributor to the central EU budget, that budget will be diverted to countries with economies wrecked by EMU. Either we accept that and attempt to adjust the rebate to compensate, or we remove ourselves from the central budget.

Secondly, a reduction of the costs of membership is not enough. Increasing (or still less, holding onto) the rebate only solves part of the problem and leaves an issue that other member states have already demonstrated they see as a canker (or, in the French case, cynically treat as a useful diversionary tactic and thus create one).

Thirdly, achieving a pledge to review EU spending issues is demonstrably not enough, as the Blair rebate deal proves at considerable cost.

Fourthly, the issue of UK tax take by Brussels is an historically mismanaged weapon that the Foreign Office has for too long been afraid to deploy. If the FCO is not up to the job, the Treasury should take the lead in the UK's renegotiations instead. We should be quite prepared to suspend our fortnightly payments to the EU treasury, which lest we forget currently run at *two thirds of a billion pounds every fortnight*. Given the scale of our net, and our gross, contributions, coupled with the realities underpinning RAL payments, this means we have increased leverage in our negotiations. Once we step outside of our normal budgetary discussions and away from the world of QMV and MEP interference, the renegotiations start to open up entirely new areas of empowerment.

Brussels, and the other EU members round the table, needs our money. If we are to let them have it, at the very least we should sell it dear.

5

Cutting Loose

Business regulation

> **Bottom lines up front**
>
> - Because of the UK's status as a global-trading low-regulation economy, it does badly from the EU's red tape and protectionism.
> - The entire UK economy pays the cost of implementing rules in fact covering just one tenth of it.
> - This burden sets it apart from most other EU economies that are far more dependent on their neighbours and can absorb EU red tape.
> - The Commission has repeatedly demonstrated it doesn't understand and can't cut red tape.

The UK's primary objective in operating in an EU environment is to secure access to European markets. Indeed, it can be legitimately argued that this is its sole objective, and that other forms of association (which could quite reasonably occur as outside associates) is political trade-off.

This then leaves Whitehall and Westminster with a quandary.

We have reviewed the cost of EU membership in silver above. But there is in addition to these membership fees a cost paid in gold – and of which gold plating is merely the finish supplied by our own civil servants.

EU rules are intended to facilitate trade between countries by simplifying intra-EU exports. The payoff for this is that administrative burdens are introduced to regulate such issues as recognisable quality, welfare, safety, 'fairness', and an increasing array of abstracts that over the decades have less to do with paperwork at borders and more to do with social engineering.[1] Be that as it may, such rules are also designed to act as quality controls so that goods can transit borders by reducing or removing the need for checks there.

What this does of course is, firstly, to standardise ('harmonise') regulations and with them costs; secondly, it standardises enforcement, though actual enforcement varies depending on the capability and intent of the member state to enforce given rules; and thirdly, since such regulations carry cost when supplementing existing rules, it adds a measure of extra expense to the businesses affected.

The problem is that the UK is disproportionately affected by these costs compared with the export advantages gained. The figures vary depending on how you assess them, but essentially somewhere between seven tenths and four fifths of the UK economy is internal, with businesses in say Sheffield trading with businesses in Liverpool; a tenth is world exports, unaffected by the single market; and the remainder is to the single market.[2] That suggests a tenth of the UK economy benefits from access to the single market. However, since red tape does not discriminate, that means that 100 per cent of the economy has to pay the costs.[3]

For a country that relies on exporting to the EU for a sizeable part of its GDP, this may be viewed as a price worth paying. But the UK is not landlocked in the centre of Europe, with a small beholden economy, dependent on EU-based multinationals, reliant on re-exporting finished products back to the EU, or focused on factories a few miles from a land border. It is, tellingly after outer-rim island economies Cyprus and Malta, the country with the lowest proportion of GDP associated with and therefore dependent on exports to the EU. Correspondingly, it is the only significant EU member state economy liable to lose more than it gains from current EU membership terms.[4]

The central question is therefore whether the value of the total EU red tape burden across the economy exceeds the value of the increased trade arising from single market access. It also invites one to consider whether the relative costs and benefits might be better rebalanced using a different form of single market arrangement. We'll return to that later. But let's focus here on the costs, since much effort will inevitably be expended on trying to assuage them.[5]

There are several estimates of the costs of single market regulations. Open Europe estimated in 2009 that the cumulative cost of regulations introduced over the previous decade in the UK, and which had their origins in the EU, was as high as £106.6bn. These estimates were subsequently updated in 2010, with a report based on over 2,300 of the government's own Impact Assessments. They found that regulation introduced between 1998 and 2009 had cost the UK economy a cumulative £176bn by 2009. Of this amount, £124bn (71 per cent) had its origin in EU legislation. Meanwhile, the British Chambers of Commerce (BCC) 'Burdens Barometer' (2010) calculated that the total gross cost of regulations introduced since 1998 was £88.3bn, £11bn higher than 2009 and compared with just £10bn in 2001. 31.2 per cent of the cumulative cost (£27.55bn) was attributable to domestic legislation, whilst 68.8 per cent (£60.75bn) was attributable to EU legislation. The most expensive regulations to date were: the Working Time Regulations 1999 (EU) at £17.8bn, the Vehicle Excise Duty (reduced pollution), amendment regulations 2000 (EU) at £10.4bn, and the Data Protection Act 1998 (EU) at £8.0bn.

The best that can be said of these figures is that they very much fall at the lower end of the scale in terms of assessed red tape costs, and exclude such issues as opportunity loss.

They also ignore the way in which the EU's regulatory framework operates as a clothes horse for Whitehall's own activism. British governments have adopted the EU's climate change and energy policies with particular zeal. Indeed the Climate Change Act (2008) insisted that UK reductions by 2020 should be more draconian than the EU's, a model described as 'leading by example'. The British government has also signed up to a 15 per cent renewables target by 2020 under the Renewables Directive which, given the low level of energy consumption sourced from renewables in the UK in the 2000s, is by far the most demanding target for any major EU country. The British government has also announced a carbon price floor in order to underpin the price of carbon, starting 2013. The costs of pursuing these policies is enormous.[6]

The physical volume of rules alone is revealing. In this parliament alone just as at late 2013, a total of 3,580 regulations and directives had been passed by the EU that affect British businesses. The total word count of all these regulations was over 13 million words (13,321,530 words). It would have taken a UK business person, working an average 40 hours a week and reading at the average reading speed of 300 words per minute, 92 days to read all the EU red tape enacted since the government came to power.[7]

Where the UK finds regulations to be onerous, it is no longer best placed to avoid them. As we have seen, Britain has just a twelfth of the votes in the Council of the European Union for deciding legislation passed by Qualified Majority Voting (QMV). It has a tenth of the MEPs (even if they were united), and a twentieth of staff in the Commission, who in any case tend to be at best passive-integrationist.[8] There is now very little economic legislation subject to a veto; taxation being one of the few categories. The UK's ability to block legislation it does not like is extraordinarily weak. It will, over time, get weaker.

Correspondingly we should not be surprised if a growing EU red tape burden will further exacerbate our membership deficit. The UK often masks its defeats by abstaining in votes or gaining a face-saving derogation, delaying the impact for another minister or government to take the flak. Even so, and despite likely knowing the QMV ballot maths in advance, UKREP makes a point of registering its opposition on average three times a year by voting formally against a measure and being defeated.[9] These include big budget issues such as unviable limits on car emissions.

In a reply to Lord Stevens (June 2006), who had asked how much UK legislation had its origins in EU legislation, Lord Triesman estimated 'that around half of all UK legislation with an impact on business, charities and the voluntary sector stems from legislation agreed by Ministers in Brussels'.

Lord Triesman's rough-and-ready 'rule of thumb' estimate of 50 per cent is of supreme significance. It means that the British government, even on its own figures, is currently hamstrung over half the legislation affecting business and the economy.

Significantly, businesses themselves now have major doubts about the value of the single market with its regulations. According to a Business for Britain survey – by 46 per cent to 37 per cent – they indicated that the costs of complying outweighed the benefits that it provided.[10] It may well be that not all red tape will be removed for UK businesses. Product regulations would have to remain. But the remainder could be lifted with a treaty deal that focused on market access not EU membership. Meanwhile, as we have seen, UK law makers would regain direct control and power of veto in world trade bodies such as UNECE where many of these regulations are actually drafted in the first place.[11]

This is the wider context of the document setting out the 30 recommendations reached by the Business Taskforce.[12] The basic principles that the group set out are valuable: the acronym they use is COMPETE, and the principles would admit of a new competitiveness test; one-in/one-out; measuring Impact Assessments; proportionality; exemptions and lighter regimes; a target for burden reduction; and evaluation of existing legislation before adding to it.

The taskforce also suggests a number of specific regulations identified as needing scaling back from or binning. Examples include removing SMEs from the provisions of the Health and Safety Framework Directive; some loosening of the Acquired Rights Directive; and exempting SMEs from incidental coverage by the Waste Framework Directive.[13]

In essence the taskforce is largely about creating opt-outs for small businesses across all EU legislation; and setting up trip wires for the Commission when it is considering bad laws. The first approach might just work. As a negotiating gain it could produce benefits to the UK economy in the order of a couple of billion pounds, and similar gains proportionately to other EU states. As a take away from any negotiations, it is at least a couple of hundred grams of weight on the scales – not enough in its own right but a start.

But why stop there? A responsive approach might call for legislative cuts at a rate of one in and two out, and carrying a minimum equivalent burden cost. They could demand a minimum of a six month default delay between anything being physically sent to parliaments and the time it is published in the Official Journal and becomes law, in order to increase scrutiny time and opportunities especially during recesses. The Commission could be required to annually publish a cost assessment of all recently enacted legislation, by Directorate General. Costs would include a range of estimates and a reasonable minimum and a maximum. A monthly online counter would be set up on the Commission's website to show running totals, operating like an updated debt clock.

Government departments in Whitehall would demonstrate the principle by leading the way and setting up their own red tape tallies too. They would also make a point of indicating wherever legislation was sourced from an EU original, list all additions and changes to the original, and show both the original Commission and amended Whitehall red tape costs. These measures could be implemented tomorrow unilaterally.

The problem with the proposals that affect the Commission, however, is basically that of experience coupled with cynicism. Attempts to curtail the legislative programme in such ways have explicitly been tried before, and even with an enthusiastic commissioner like Günter Verheugen on board have stalled. The problem is one of selfish civil service prerogative, coupled with the motor of European integrationism that allows for no political retrogression. COMPETE, simply put, requires a civil service that's prepared to implement it; and the Eurocracy has rejected it in the past. Worse, it pretends it hasn't.

Subsidiarity is the classic example of a subverted safeguard. But the reform agenda itself, pushed after the scandals of the Santer Commission and by failed referenda, has been attempted and has fallen by the wayside.

The Commission's REFIT programme – covering codification, recasting, repeal, sunset clauses, and revision – already exists to achieve this better governance objective and has done now for several years. The sad reality is that it fails to do so. A stocktake in 2009 produced a paltry 14 obsolete measures in the CFP that could be repealed 'for reasons of legal security and clarity'. These included one item of legislation that was an interim measure for projects for 1982; one interim measure for 2001; one that covered a period around 2001 for an agreement from 1999 that then ended; one was intended to cover just 2003, another just 2004, and a third just 2006; one related to the aftermath of an oil spill in 2002; three were for a transitional period after Spain joined; three were succeeded by another directive covering in part the same thing; and one was an interim measure for the former East Germany after unification.[14] The examples chosen for cutting red tape do not suggest anyone was enthusiastically slashing the red tape with anything other than a butter knife.

Nor have matters improved since. In REFIT's latest format, the Commission announced it intended to merely review 50 existing legislative items, also using the exercise as an excuse to bin another 50 that had failed anyway to get legislative agreement across the EU institutions.

This comes as the size of the *acquis communautaire* constantly expands. Estimates vary. Official EU sources referred to 95,000 pages in the mid 1990s, and 105,000 pages by 2004. A 2005 review by Open Europe suggested the real figure was actually closer to 170,000, since two thirds of a million pages had been churned out since the EEC was first created and around a quarter of them were still active.[15] That figure excluded other paperwork not printed in the Official Journal 'L' series, and excluded material coming out of the ECJ.

More tellingly, of that figure, around 100,000 pages alone had been generated over the previous decade: the paper machine was accelerating wildly. We can predict a similar quantity has been produced in the decade since, particularly with the expansion of EU treaty competences.

The Commission is not responsive to reforms that limit its power; the European Parliament is not responsive to reforms that limit European integration, even before getting onto the politics of social welfare issues or MEPs' pet projects; the members of the European Council are collectively minded to veto on principle what roll back does come through.

Consequently, we can only underline that the *acquis* is so named for a deliberate purpose. It is intended to be permanent and immutable. Attempts to dissolve it will require a complete change in the structure, intent, and fabric of the European Commission. That is not going to happen under a Commission President whom Mr Cameron himself has identified as an obstacle to reform. Redirecting the Commission away from the integrationist rocks requires a captain with a real 'appetite for change', and the Prime Minister himself has stated that Mr Juncker does not possess that hunger. It will take a truly tectonic shift in the renegotiation to budge the Commission away from the guardian of the treaties, and into becoming the guardian of prosperity. It requires other countries to permanently give up on closer integration in future years, and that is not the consensus view.

Trade with the rest of the world

> **Bottom lines up front**
>
> - The EU is becoming less important as an export market over time.
> - This is partly self-inflicted, and thus shared with the UK.
> - The UK can get round this by either moving to a single-market-but-not-EU status; or by moving fully outside the customs union and negotiating low tariff deals. Both are viable but more official figures are needed.
> - Staying put is not a strategic option.

The International Monetary Fund (IMF)'s database goes back to 1980, when the EU28's share of world GDP (significantly, in market exchange rate terms) was over 33 per cent. That of the US was over 28 per cent, and China's a paltry 3 per cent. The EU28, as it would become, formed the biggest economic bloc in the world.

Today, the margin between the EU and the US has disappeared. The EU's share in 2012 was down to 23 per cent, barely ahead of the US's 22.5 per cent. But the 'EU28 *excluding the UK*', relevant when talking about the 'market' for UK exports, was under 20 per cent, clearly down on the US's 22.5 per cent. That of course means, incidentally, that the mantra of the EU being (just about) the 'biggest single market in the world' is no longer true when we are talking about our 'biggest single export market.'

It will become even less true over time. The IMF currently expects the EU-UK share to slip further by 2019. Germany's annual average growth rate is expected to be 1.45 per cent from 2014–19, contrasted with the UK at 2.5 per cent, and the US at 2.75 per cent. The decline in the EU's relative share of world output reflects its poor growth prospects as well as the rise of the emerging markets. Growth in the Eurozone in the first quarter of 2014 was very disappointing.

Likewise, in purchasing power parities terms, the EU28's share was 30.4 per cent in 1980, 19.2 per cent in 2012 and the IMF expects it to be 16.7 per cent in 2019.

Moreover, further out the demographics look bleak for some key European countries. The UN's latest population projections show that Europe's population made up nearly 22 per cent of the world total in 1950, dropping to around 11 per cent in 2010, and is expected to be about 7.5 per cent in 2050 and less than 6 per cent in 2100. More specifically, Germany's demographics are among the most adverse of any major country, alongside Japan, Korea and several Eastern European countries (including Russia and Poland). According to UN data Germany's total population, in general, and working population, in particular, are already falling. Having peaked at nearly 84 million in 2004, it was 83 million in 2010 and may drop to about 73 million by 2050 and 57 million by 2100.

Incidentally the demographics in the UK and France are very different from Germany's. The UN expects both countries to have populations of 73 million in 2050, similar to Germany, with further growth to the end of the century. Populations in Italy and Spain by contrast are also projected to fall by 2100.

So as we plan for how our trade may be facilitated, we need to ensure that we are not destructively hobbled to a customs union whose format limits our exports on other global markets. We are once more reminded of the celebrated Gillray cartoon with Pitt and Napoleon dividing up the world between them.[16]

An intriguing dynamic in this is the increasing force of integrated supply chains. In effect, these are merely an extension of what Adam Smith discussed, and are now known as Global Value Chains (GVCs): where production crosses borders to add value. Indeed, at a basic level this was what colonial trade was all about. However, the system today is now considerably more developed. A typical manufacturing company today uses inputs from more than 35 different contractors across the world.[17] The increase in GVCs means that one country's gross exports increasingly rely on significant intermediate imports from other countries and, therefore, the value-added (VA) by industries in 'upstream' countries. A good example is the iPod. In reality, only 10 per cent of a 'made in China' iPod might be 'value-added' in China. The bulk of the components are imported from Japan, with much of the rest from the US and Korea. If it ends up being sold in America, the finished product is thus a re-export back. The conventional trade figures on which we extol so much of our trade with the single market do not make allowances for the import content of exports. They can exaggerate exports' contribution to GDP. In the case of that Chinese iPod, 100 per cent of an exported iPod is recorded as a Chinese gross export, contributing to GDP. But in value-added terms only 10 per cent of the iPod export contributed to GDP. The economically significant concept is how much of the export is 'value-added' (or domestically produced) in China.

They can also distort a country's bilateral export share. For example, 100 per cent of that same 'Chinese' iPod exported to the US goes into the calculation of the US share of Chinese gross exports. But in value-added terms (allowing for intermediate imports), the US share of Chinese exports is likely to be significantly different – and lower.

The OECD (with the WTO) has done some fascinating and very important work on trade in value-added, allowing for the intermediate import content in exports, for 2009. The findings were significant, and put UK-EU trade relationships in quite a different light from conventional accounts. In 2009 the share going to the EU was 48 per cent in the conventional accounts. In value-added terms the share dropped to 41 per cent for 2009.

Moreover, because only a proportion (83 per cent, 2009 figure) of our exports is domestically value-added by being domestically produced, the exports/GDP ratio drops from 28.4 per cent to 23.5 per cent. Note further that exports were depressed in 2009, owing to the Great Recession. The exports to the EU/GDP ratio was estimated around 14 per cent on the conventional accounts in 2009, which drops to under 10 per cent in value-added.[18]

The more you look at the data, the less important the EU is to UK exports and to UK GDP. That trend is further exacerbated by the enduring sickliness of the Eurozone.

Unsurprisingly, our EU-orientated share of exports of goods and services fell from 55 per cent (2002) to 45 per cent (2012) and 44.5 per cent in 2013, using the conventional trade accounts. The largest market of destination in 2012 was the US (17 per cent), followed by Germany (less than 9 per cent).

Clearly the UK is forging ahead in non-EU markets, despite the much vaunted 'attractions' of the single market and the EU's customs union. Of course, trade with non-EU markets similarly has to conform to the importing countries' product regulations and deal with their customs procedures. But Britain's exporters are perfectly capable of handling these matters successfully. Similarly, non-EU exporters to the EU are perfectly capable of trading successfully with the EU, without being in either the single market or the customs union, underlining the fact that EU membership is quite unnecessary to trade with the EU.

It's also useful to note that some of the UK's most successful trading partners do not have special trade agreements with the EU. These include the USA (where a Transatlantic Trade and Investment Partnership is still being sorted out), Canada (where an FTA, 'CETA' has only just recently been negotiated and is not yet ratified), Australia, the Gulf States, China and Japan.

A comparison of the UK's geographical trade patterns (for goods) with Germany and Switzerland shows that Britain's export share to the EU was not just lower than Germany's (57.4 per cent) but also non-EU Switzerland's (55.5 per cent) in 2012.[20] On this criterion the Swiss economy was more integrated with the EU than Britain's. Perhaps this is not so surprising given Switzerland's geographical position, but it does suggest that non-membership of the EU is no barrier to trade.

A shift in global perceptions has facilitated this. When we joined the EEC back in 1973, Europe was a low tariff, growing region. But across the world now, tariffs are now generally low and the EU is no longer growing very much. But even on accession, the Treasury was sceptical. As Hugo Young observed, the Treasury remained officially against British entry: its judgement of the economic consequences was negative, and it submitted a paper to that effect.[21]

Into this mix we can also add the reality of our running a sizeable deficit in goods and services with other EU countries. It was £54bn in 2013 – a goods deficit of £65bn, partly offset by a services surplus of just £11bn.

Looking ahead the prospects for many Commonwealth countries, and therefore the UK's trade with them, appear very positive. In particular, the modern Commonwealth contains over two billion people and accounts for 15 per cent of world GNI in PPP terms. It spans five continents and contains developed, emerging and developing economies. In its diversity it captures the character of the 21st century globalised economy as nearly every major economic grouping is represented.

Commonwealth countries have favourable demographics and, insofar as economic growth is correlated with growth in the working population, their growth prospects are positive. Several of the countries have deep reserves of key natural resources.

Reflecting shared history and commonalities of language, law and business practice, it has been estimated that Commonwealth countries trading with one another experience business costs 10–15 per cent lower than similar dealings with non-Commonwealth countries of comparable size and GDP. This has been called the 'Commonwealth Effect' or the 'Commonwealth Advantage'.[22]

In sum, the need is essentially one of measuring relative benefit from the three options that should be under consideration: continuing EU membership with further opt-outs, or shifting to single market membership under skeletal terms, or being outside of the customs union and trading in from the global marketplace. Each has benefits and costs. But civil servants should already be analysing the competitive advantage arising from each of these models, what the economic risks are, what benefits are replicated under international trading rules, and what new freedoms accrue to investment and to individual sectors.

Only by understanding these differences can negotiators even begin to assess the framework that the new treaty needs to take – building up or knocking down.

The inference is that full EU membership on anything resembling current terms carries inescapable business costs that will destroy our global competitiveness over a generation; that membership even of simply a rarefied customs union retains many costs (especially the inability to negotiate our own trade deals); while the 'door ajar' principle of trading into the single market on mutually preferential terms is likely to be the best option, if key sectoral interests can be safeguarded (as indeed seems likely given the UK trade deficit with the EU, and the existence of UK businesses as part of EU GVCs – like Rolls Royce engines in Airbus for instance).

This last approach on review will likely prove to be the best one, a clothes-peg approach of putting mutually-agreed items on a line bilaterally. In plain English, we agree to just trade with one another. However, of the options this also remains politically the most contentious. The mathematics remain burdened with uncertainties owing to a lack of detailed official analysis.[23] Whitehall ministries are afraid to switch on the light.

So unfortunately, it remains taboo to consider that a country doesn't actually need to be an EU member as we think of it today, even for a country like Switzerland which is more closely integrated with its neighbours than ours is. It remains a particular paradox that the costs inherent in the single market structure (let alone full membership) are such a significant burden across all of UK business, yet both have for so long remained politically sacrosanct. The very detail that a customs union has outside walls that hamper egress to the world beyond them is typically forgotten. Until we get our collective political heads around these realities though, we are not going to be in a position to strike the best deal for this country in our renegotiations.[24]

The worst aspect is that our time is limited, even without the framework of a referendum to bring into consideration. The Eurozone, assuming it's over its existential crisis and that it survives for the foreseeable future, will continue to integrate. Life for EU countries outside the Eurozone, the big project, will change and their influence decline. Eurozone integration is an accelerating game-changer. The status quo is not an option.

Localism

Bottom lines up front

- Powers restored to national control needn't sit at Westminster.
- The CFP is part of a wider plan to federalise a common maritime area, and needs to come back to national/regional control.

> - The CAP also needs to come back to national control. There needs to be a national debate on setting up a vastly smaller replacement scheme suitable for both consumers and producers.

Localism as a concept is firmly on the UK political agenda, thanks to policing reform, directly-elected mayors, the right of recall debate, and the debate and negotiations on the future of Scotland. Its principles might also be applied to the discussions on our future form of association with the EU.

The skeleton form of the EEC was one with a pyramid structure, tapering upwards to Brussels. This lent itself to builders slapping on ever more accretions to the model. Then came the idea of subsidiarity, but this half-assumed that a federal model was right and that a number of major powers did deserve to be cemented in at Brussels. It was an idea that also meant extending the precinct at the pyramid base, since the priests would still keep watch over all they surveyed. What is needed now is a clean rupture between what our association covers, and what it does not.

Renegotiations need to be about more than ending a directive or amending a regulation to provide an opt-out. It needs to physically re-order the architecture by restoring, in full and in permanence, key titles and chapters to UK national control.

Once these powers are restored, that should not be the end of the matter. Good governance requires further thought on how and where powers could be pushed further down to local communities – not simply whether to Edinburgh or Cardiff, and certainly not in order to play voodoo with Prescottian regional government, but in terms of building up local community responsibility and engagement.

Foremost in this list should be repeal of the Common Fisheries Policy. The management of fishing grounds has been so patently disastrous, we should hardly be expected to have to expand on the extent of the scandal.

The policy was invented on the eve of the accession of the Atlantic states of the UK, Ireland and Denmark, and with the expectation of Norway also joining. In the event, the Norwegian fishing minister resigned in protest and the resulting scandal blew their referendum out of the water, as it were. That still left other North Sea fishing grounds opened up and remaining national waters at risk from a repeatedly expiring ten year derogation. But the entire premise of including fisheries in the first place was founded on a pretence that fish were covered in the basic treaties when in fact only landed fish as products and foodstuffs were. It might justifiably be described as the original sin of the EEC.

Those wanting to delve deeper into the dire history that followed could usefully re-examine the material formerly produced by the excellent campaigners at *Save Britain's Fish*.[25] It might be useful just to highlight a couple of details that another cost audit of the CFP has been able to come up with.[26] It estimated that the economic cost of the CFP ran at £2.81bn annually. This appears to be an impossible sum until one considers the impact the policy has had on an entire industry, on the industries that service it, and the supply chain it supports, and on the communities themselves. That £2.81bn came from costs arising from unemployment in the fleet and in support industries (£138m), decline in the coastal communities (£27m), pending damage coming to the recreational fishing industry (low estimate used, £11m), the UK share of support to foreign fishing fleets under EU grants (£64m), the UK share of support to foreign fisheries industry under EU grants (£1m), the redeemable UK share of EU third water fishing permits (allowing for half to be invested in development aid: £12m), loss of comparative competitiveness (£10m), ongoing decommissioning schemes (£4m), foreign-flagged UK vessels (£15m), administrative burden (£22m), economic cost of loss of access to home waters under 200 nautical mile principle (£2.11bn), higher food prices (factored into social security payments, £269m – and meaning an additional £186 per household a year at the checkout), and the economic value of tens of thousands of dumped fish (£130m). The single biggest cost is the opportunity cost of surrendering the resource that other countries retain as a national asset, but which we have allowed to pool – and then subsidised our major competitors using UK taxpayer money.

The Blair-Santer deal in 1997, supposedly establishing an economic obligation on quota hoppers, was a sham.[27] As Greenpeace regularly point out, five of the ten largest UK-registered trawlers are not British at all. The largest, the *Cornelis Vrolijk*, reportedly lands its catch in the Netherlands. Its take alone is equivalent to the entire Cornish fleet, or around a fifth of the entire English TAC. With a displacement just short of 5,000t, this industrial fishing vessel is on a par with a modern Royal Navy frigate. Those elements of the fleet that do remain domestically dominated, the under 30' fleet, are increasingly outpaced and (thanks to a comparative lack of past upgrade subsidies) antiquated and underpowered by comparison with their continental counterparts.

This is before we even mention the ecological aspects of this broken system, with the impact of mismanaged stocks, hecatomb dumping of surplus-to-quota fish, and also cetacean bycatch. The fundamental problem is similar to that of fraud: no one owns the policy just as no one feels a responsibility for embezzled money, making it someone else's resource to be exploited.

The EU has supposedly launched a series of reforms, which came into force at the start of 2014. The reality is however that this allows for regional consultation, which in practice already happened, and for all the countries involved in a fishery to jointly consult with the Commission.

The North Sea is one of seven areas to have gained a formal Advisory Council. It has 40 members and 24 members of the executive. But reflect on the participants for a moment. Of the latter, four are Euroquangos; two represent fishing groups for countries that don't even border the North Sea (and which under accession terms weren't meant to gain extra access in the first place); and the two British fishing representatives (both Scottish, incidentally) have the same level of representation as anglers and fewer than wildlife and environment campaigners.[28]

The CFP is broken. Any mechanism that takes 15 years to agree to change the size of a mesh to reduce catch of juveniles is fundamentally flawed and beyond saving. The CFP needs to be binned and national control restored, so that local communities gain real input and responsibility. International organisations such as the North Atlantic Fisheries Organisation (NAFO) already exist to which the UK would re-accede as a full voting member in its own right (absurdly, with the EU represented as a bloc, NAFO has twelve members – of which one is Ukraine, while France gets its own seat thanks to Saint Pierre et Miquelon). Owen Paterson's extensive research, undertaken while on the Opposition Front Bench, already demonstrates the opportunities on offer from following the bilateralism of Norway and Iceland, focused on eco-management rather than political barter. This can be further built on by delegating responsibilities downwards to regional and community control.

But that is not the whole story. There is another reason why the UK needs to be outside of the CFP, and this is a fundamental part of the whole renegotiation dynamic. Fisheries constitutes just one aspect of a broader plan for wider integration, and demonstrates how small losses of sovereignty in seemingly unconnected areas add up to massive and intended shifts in political power.

The EU has a broader unifying maritime policy. It has already on several occasions attempted to assume control over North Sea energy. During the drafting of the EU Constitution, this escalated into a major diplomatic row thanks to a late insert to the draft that the *Daily Telegraph* picked up, that would have extended competences over oil and gas rigs, a move which the Commission had tried before but had been seen off through unanimity. Since then, it has successfully pushed Directive 2013/30/EU, inserting Commission authority on the basis of the environmental impact of a disaster. This is entirely in keeping with the Commission's declared intent as set out in its Green Paper of 2006, *Towards a Future Maritime Policy for the Union* (2006/0275).[29] This covered, for instance, renewable energy, shipyards and other infrastructure, cyclones, immigration, fisheries management (long seen as best achieved through a common European fleet), nutrition in seafood, environmental disasters such as those generated by oil slicks, port management, sea lanes (and therefore Dover Control), flag registers, maritime accident investigations, maritime research, dredging, climate change, coastal defences, terrorist threats, tourism, maritime surveillance, angling, smuggling, trafficking, piracy, naval defence, the coastguard, search and rescue, heritage (including museums, and underwater archaeology), yachting, and so on.[30]

Frankly put, for as long as the UK is a part of the Common Fisheries Policy, all of these are at risk from being run by Brussels.[31] The UK would be by default accepting the premise that there should be a Common Maritime Policy, constituting the above. Lift any item from that list, and the Commission is already planning a common policy around it. If it floats, swims, scuttles or rusts, it will increasingly be managed elsewhere – unless we extricate ourselves from the CFP, and even then that is no watertight guarantee.[32]

The importance of disapplying the CFP has been recognised by the Conservative Party in the past, with several front benchers adopting the policy of withdrawal from it. Including it on the renegotiation package now in absolutist terms is therefore merely revisiting a previously accepted norm.[33] If countries such as Norway and Canada are able to manage their fisheries effectively, responsibly and responsively outside of the CFP, then a maritime and fishing nation such as the UK should be able to as well.

Another key item worthy of repatriation on localist grounds is that of the Common Agricultural Policy. This is an overarching policy whose remit encompasses everything between the sun-baked volcanic rocks of the Canaries to the frozen tundra of elf-filled Lapland. It is a *dirigiste* affair whose specs are tailored to keep Frenchmen on their hills by means of billions of euros worth of belated German reparations.

The problem for the UK is that the UK has somehow been drawn into the repayments scheme – and on a massive scale. The UK could operate an identical scheme but just covering British farmers and save a billion pounds overnight.

The optimal solution would be for the renegotiators to agree to restore CAP spending to national exchequers. That would invigorate reformers within each country to address the system's many failings and inherent waste. Unfortunately, there are too many vested interests to realistically expect this to happen.

Our target should therefore be a variable CAP, with the UK extricated from the CAP budget, and with London being able to establish a set of subsidy rules according to what the public wants. We can anticipate this would be a gradual shift towards subsidy for subsistence, marginal and hill farms; support for 'heritage' environments; emergency backing for pressurised stock during a particular slump; special provision for isolated communities at risk of critical and unsustainable depopulation[34]; 'sponsorship' for cultivation of items socially valued but economically unviable[35]; and such like. The fundamental principle though would be that these would be the focus of a wide debate based on need and policy priorities, perhaps reviewing very localised priorities and exceptional needs, rather than just doled out from the public purse again as uncosted political favours to any lobby.

This then raises the question as to how the UK's agricultural imports from other EU countries would then work. To which the answer is: as openly or as constrained as access to and from and across the single market more widely works, except that the French would now be obliged to take UK trading access extremely seriously. Paris would be subject to an extremely vociferous domestic lobby keen to maintain its export market and existing levels of access to UK consumers.

The UK will have an astonishing range of options available to it if we quit the CAP. At one end of the scale, if we step away from the agricultural part of the EU customs union, it allows the option of opening up UK imports to the global market and reducing the agricultural tariffs the EU forces on us. This allows for cheaper prices at the till, and indeed considerable saving.

Some figures may here help. A review by the TaxPayers' Alliance has costed the CAP for Britain.[36] There is an increased cost of food prices of £5.3bn, or £398 per household every year; increased social welfare costs of £317m; an estimated £264m in regulatory burdens; £5m from unnecessary duplication of food safety agencies; £4.7bn as the UK share of the CAP budget; and removing double counting from agriculture and sugar levies in both EU budgetary contributions and higher prices at the till, that makes for an end cost to the UK of £10.3bn a year. As we have indicated, at least £1bn of that bill could go upon quitting the CAP, and much more if we decide to stop running a protectionist market and transition like New Zealand did to a free trade model (or at least, part of the way there).

Consequently, revoking CAP membership must be another key negotiating term. This will achieve the triple objectives of reducing the net bill from EU membership; reducing the cost of living for ordinary families (for whom food prices form a major part of their budget, and who would notice it most); and increasing the diplomatic ability of the UK to negotiate a better trade deal with the EU states, since it generates a direct incentive for the most obstructionist of them to come to fair terms with the UK on trade matters if these talks drag on.[37] It also has other effects, particularly in support of third world producers since the EU's external tariffs make much of their produce uncompetitive (they are currently designed to do precisely that).

Quitting the CAP and CFP aspects of the EU deal are just two measures with localist appeal. They are also not new ideas. During the Convention on the Future of Europe, one of the submissions specifically observed:

> Many policies now run from Brussels have demonstrably failed when run as part of a collective. These must be repatriated. To this end, the Convention should debate which areas are best run by national or – where appropriate – regional assemblies. Fisheries is a prime example, and both CAP and development aid stand little chance of meaningful reform while collectivised. As a rule of thumb, matters which do not cross borders or affect the single market for other countries should be left for the local authorities to deal with. Brussels must become less of a government, and more of an arbiter.

This was signed by a number of elder statesmen from across Europe, including future foreign secretary William Hague, at that time a backbencher.[38] Even if this concept runs too far against the grain of collectivist ever closer union to achieve multilateral agreement, such pared off terms can be met through a bilateral treaty outside of full EU membership.[39]

Of course, there are other areas where the localist agenda could win widespread support. Mechanisms might be set in place that could help identify case studies where local communities have been damaged by distant Brussels decisions or consequences, especially by bad or vanity grants. The cause of localism could be bolstered by ingenious development of a bad grants website, allowing local campaigners to flag up existing and threatened failures in order to better redirect spending into more effective routes. True localism would also undermine the dangerous example of the 'sock puppets', Brussels-sponsored lobbyists lobbying the Commission to do more on their behalf: 'Brussels talking to Brussels' as it was styled by David Heathcoat-Amory during the European Convention.[40]

But 60 years of experience demonstrates that the EU has the turning circle of an asteroid. In these areas as in others, the only prospect for enduring change comes when such competences are removed from the UK's treaties with the EU, and transformed into issues of domestic debate and management.

7

Planning

The magic 8-ball

> **Bottom lines up front**
> - Renegotiators need to review a wide range of Eurosceptic work. The subject is so massive only a ranging study will begin – collectively – to address the key points.
> - Eight key texts deserve particular study.

Any paper seeking to fully explore the intricacies of the EU treaties will face increasing technical difficulties because of the Marianas Trench depths of complexity involved. The best we can do is to identify the salient areas and allow the negotiators further opportunities to delve into the key waters.

With that in mind we here point to a handful of critical research publications that go into essential aspects in far greater detail. Any review of the functioning of EU treaty systems and global economics becomes extremely complex very quickly. It is correspondingly just as easy for commentators – particularly politicians – to nominate one end state (say, Swiss-style membership) and declare that all will be well by generating ourselves into such a condition overnight. The reality is far more complicated because of the mass of legacy circuitry that will remain connected following any change, as well as the huge amounts of unseen trade and treaty wiring now connecting the global economy.

Collectively, we would therefore recommend the following eight papers as an ensemble. Combined, they constitute a constructive way through this quantum confusion, acting as a route to developing the in-depth answers those renegotiating the treaties need to find before they start. There are different models. Indeed, some offer different formats for solutions. But as one of the papers itself explores, there is no such thing as a single silver bullet, but a range of possible responses with varying benefits whose appeal differs from country to country.

(I) *Terms of Endearment: What Powers Would David Cameron Need to Repatriate to Make EU Association Work*, TaxPayers' Alliance

This paper does what it says on the tin.[1] It explains how minor changes made during any nugatory renegotiation would not last, given the onward-rolling direction of the EU blob. It gives ten past examples of other EU states playing hard ball over EU treaty negotiations, demonstrating that it is a legitimate tactic. It explores how the Conservative Party has a track record in demanding certain areas should be repatriated, so any dismantling of key aspects of our treaty of association would be entirely in keeping with past policies. It also demonstrates how, time after time, deals are trumpeted as victories only to unravel within hours of a Prime Minister's return.

The paper adopts a jigsaw approach, identifying 20 solutions. If only two or three were adopted, a result would at least be visible: a large number and the end picture becomes more and more meaningful. The list is in Table 7.1, below.

Table 7.1: TPA's Recommended Jigsaw Pieces for the Negotiations

Number	Item	Comment
1	End to 'ever closer union'	Not just deleting the term but removing the passerelle and 'rubber' clauses (and intent)[2]
2	Return CAP to national control	
3	Return CFP to national control	
4	Cut the contribution	
5	Re-establish the social chapter opt-out	
6	Reduce ECJ 'imperial' status	ECJ supremacy is currently challenged by several EU states (including Germany), but set out in the Lisbon Treaty and by EU case law
7	Return international development to national control	
8	Step back from EU defence integration	Use NATO and bilaterals instead
9	Bilateral tailored agreements on JHA, asylum, and immigration	
10	Withdraw from a number of pointless areas of funding, e.g. regional aid, education, culture	Flexibility to allow opting back out as preferred
11	Tax freedom, inc. over VAT	Reduce EU contribution accordingly
12	Right to bilateral trade agreements	
13	Return space programme to multilateral (non-EU) control	Subject to 'country of origin' rules
14	Push a massive reform agenda	
15–20	Six unilateral actions	Includes a cost-benefit review of membership, a Cabinet Minister assigned to review surplus *acquis* after the renegotiations, work on gold-plating and transparency, and a default scrutiny reserve

(II) *Time to Jump: A Positive Vision of a Britain Out of the EU and in EEA Lite*, **by David Campbell-Bannerman, MEP**

Campbell-Bannerman's book is based on a mass of detailed research auditing the status of the UK-EU relationship, which should have been the purview of the Balance of Competences Review. The key feature of this work however lies in the conclusion, based on a technical review of the treaties whose legality is confirmed by a professor of European Law, that a new model association could be generated that strips away vast slices of the treaties that cause the UK so much grief. To quote the author:

> These sorts of models of association are legalistic, technical and not very people-friendly, but EEA Lite is designed to sit somewhere between the successful but over-prescriptive EEA Agreement launched in 1994 post the single market and the Swiss-style set of bilateral agreements, which are far more democratic but less structured, more idiosyncratic, and less clear institutionally in terms of surveillance and dispute resolution and provide only agreed sectoral access to the EU single market through additional agreements.

In essence this is a modified form of EEA settlement involving a revised look at how the *acquis* works, and increasing greater border controls, operating under the model of the joint committees that both those systems enjoy.

The particular value of this thinking lies in its originality in adapting existing models within the framework of treaties as the text currently stands. The actual nature of the end agreement itself is of course open to subjective debate. Technically, with the terms under this arrangement the UK would no longer be 'within' the EU, and it is on the cusp of the single market itself. What also emerges from the remainder of the book is that, if it can be reached by a cooperative Council and Commission, such an approach solves a significant number of the problems. Meanwhile, it also reminds us that the issue of EU membership is both totemic and meaningless: at what point in a set of treaty terms does a state no longer count as being a member, if a particular opt-out exists or clause is disapplied? What actually counts is the value of the negotiated arrangement itself, not the title attached to it.[3]

(III) *Options for Change Green Paper: Renegotiating the UK's Relationship with the EU*, **by the Fresh Start APPG**

The current parliament has seen a serious attempt by a number of backbenchers to audit the issues, and this is very much still worthy of revisiting. To quote the authors:

> The Fresh Start Project is not about leaving the EU; it is about a fundamental renegotiation of the UK's relationship with it. We must resist any temptation among civil service negotiators to limit our focus to just one or two points in a negotiation. We need a substantial renegotiation and a shopping list of improvements and reforms to the status quo. What are important to us are matters of principle, not matters of negotiating expediency.

Fresh Start adopted a variable approach. Rather than simply generate a list, they ingeniously devised a menu. For each of the competences under consideration, they set out a number of proposals annotated with a traffic light coding.

The options for reform open to the UK were correspondingly put into three broad categories. Green represented those measures that can be achieved domestically or within the current EU legal framework. Amber meant those measures that require negotiated EU treaty change, by which was meant some relatively minor readjustment. This contrasted with the fundamental renegotiations required for the final category: red covered those steps that the UK could take unilaterally that would involve breaking its treaty obligations. The authors noted:

> In practice there is some overlap between these categories, particularly 'Green' and 'Amber' options. Many 'Green options' that are theoretically possible under the current EU legal framework would require the political agreement of other Member States and/or the EU institutions, which would be more or less difficult to achieve in individual cases. The renegotiation of individual EU Directives usually requires a qualified majority of national ministers and the agreement of the European Parliament and the European Commission, while renegotiating the EU budget requires unanimity among Member States.

Consequently, this list itself provides a key insight into the ambition surrounding the treaty talks themselves. Any deal that ends up with predominantly 'green' aspects would be easily achievable but, notwithstanding any smatterings of amber, would be a wasted opportunity. More sunset hues would be more difficult to achieve but demonstrate a truly meaningful treaty change.

Table 7.2, below, puts this balance into context though. The majority of the paper's proposals fall into the 'relatively straightforward category' taken individually. These tend to be concepts focused on individual failings, rather than wider issues running as fault lines across the treaty and EU structures. It is when there is a failure in arranging their collective reform, requiring a shift down the traffic light colour coding, that the deeper value of the document correspondingly becomes more apparent.

Table 7.2: Breakdown of Fresh Start Colour Coding Frequency by Treaty Area

Competence/Area	Green items 'continue to try to'	Amber items 'negotiate'	Red items 'If not, then'
Trade	4	2	1
Regional Development	2	1	1
CAP	4	1	1
CFP	6	1	1
Budget and institutions	4	2	1
Social and employment law	2	1	1
Financial services	6	4	1
Environment	4	2	1
Policing and criminal justice	2	3	1
Immigration	2	1	1
Defence	4	2	1

In essence, this Fresh Start paper provides the Foreign Office with a useful manual for gear box assembly.[4] It does not advise on how heavily to tread on the accelerator, which is also a key need-to-know.

(IV) *Manning the Pumps: A Handbook for Salvaging the Eurosceptic Credentials of the Conservative Party*, **by the Freedom Association**

This entire paper is relevant to this review but we shall here focus on just three particularly useful aspects.

The first is the inclusion of a formula which looks at the terms of association and the national interest.[5] It sets out five contrasting interests that offset each other through 15 contrasting and occasionally abstract areas for consideration; they essentially comprise trade, sovereignty, long term direction, peace and stability, and the alternatives on offer. What quickly becomes clear is that with different dynamics at play for different EU member states, some countries have a far greater incentive to be a part of the EU in its present form than others, while some countries will see the advantage in their terms reduce over time. (The formula is reproduced in Annex G.)

The second and third aspects are interconnected. The study identifies no fewer than 16 models of association with the EU, as set out in Table 7.3 below.

Table 7.3: Existing Forms and Models of EU Association

Category	Nature	Example	Type
0	Internal political union/merger with nation state	East Germany[6]	EU full membership
1	EU membership with full integration	France	
2	EU membership with opt-outs	UK	
3	Internal Market association outside of the EU (EEA), with options on opt-ins e.g. Schengen	Norway	Associate membership
4	Symmetric free trade agreement with bolt-ons	Switzerland	
5	Customs union, with possible fringe benefits	Turkey	Customs union
6	Deep and Comprehensive Free Trade Agreement (DCFTA)	Ukraine	Advanced trade agreement
7	Basic symmetric free trade agreement (e.g. CEFTA)	Macedonia	
8	Partnership and cooperation agreement	Tajikistan	
9	Asymmetric free trade agreement	South Africa	Basic trade agreement
10	Non-reciprocal trade preference agreement with bolt-ons	Macedonia (formerly)	
11	Global System of Preferences Plus status (GSP+)	Honduras	
12	Global System of Preferences status (GSP)	Iraq	
13	Most Favoured Nation status (MFN)	Namibia	
14	Less-than-MFN	North Korea	Restricted trade access
15	Sanctioned or embargoed state	Burma (past)	

Of itself, this list demonstrates that there is a huge amount of scope to renegotiate our terms of association to generate a bilateral agreement that is *sui generis*. More remarkable however is what happens when applying the principles of relative advantage to each of these treaty forms. It becomes evident that different treaties suit different European economies.

A key failing by those endorsing the near-*status quo* is not understanding the variety of trade terms that are today in play. In November 2014, Sir John Major appeared to be trailing possible FCO negotiation lines. On one interview, he stated that he 'would not like to be the Prime Minister in ten or twenty years' time who had to tell the Commons they had to pass into British law a number of directives over which they had no input in order to allow us to trade with them.'[7] Without being churlish and raising the QMV he himself opened the door to through Maastricht, Sir John is here rejecting not there being any alternative to EU membership, but merely one model: the Turkish one. The EEA model does generate the direct input while also cutting out the need for swathes of those directives; alternatively, the model of trading into the customs union under an FTA means that parliament does not need to pass any directives into UK law at all. It is difficult to judge the cause or motive generating this error, but it may help explain some of the politics of the early 1990s.

Following on from this, it is worth here reflecting on how the Commission itself expresses this range. One might expect perhaps a willingness to mask such divergence by applying a common and limiting set of vocabulary, perhaps applying three terms to describe the nature of the agreements being reached. In fact, the opposite is the case, with the use of an even greater variation in terms than might be expected (see Table 7.4, below). We can thus contrast the generic application of treaty forms with the even more complex and nuanced reality as the Commission itself describes its activity.

Table 7.4: Diversity of Nomenclature in EU Trade Treaties

Type of Agreement	Example
EU member state[8]	France
European Economic Area (EEA)	Norway
Cooperation and customs union (CCU)	San Marino
Customs union	Turkey
Transatlantic Trade and Investment Partnership (TTIP, pending)	USA
Comprehensive Trade and Economic Agreement (CETA, ongoing)	Canada
Free Trade Agreement plus bilateral(s)	Switzerland, Faroes
Deep and Comprehensive Free Trade Agreement (DCFTA)	Ukraine
New Generation Free Trade Agreement	Korea
Stabilisation and Association Agreement	Macedonia
Agreement on Commercial and Economic Cooperation (ACEC)	Canada (previously)
Agreement on Trade and Commercial and Economic Cooperation (ATCEC)	USSR (previously)

Type of Agreement	Example
Agreement on Trade and Economic Cooperation	Mongolia
Economic Partnership, Political Coordination and Cooperation Agreement (EPPCCA)	Mexico
Interim Agreement on Trade and Trade-related Matters	Bosnia
Trade, Development and Cooperation Agreement (ATDC)	South Africa
Free Trade Agreement	Malaysia (ongoing)
Trade Agreement	Colombia
Economic Partnership Agreement (EPA)	CARIFORUM (provisional)
Association Agreement and Additional Protocol	Chile
'Association Agreement with a strong trade component'	Central America
Europe Agreement Establishing an Association, (EEA)	Liechtenstein
Euro-Mediterranean Agreement Establishing an Association (EMAA)	Israel
Interim Partnership Agreement	Madagascar
Comprehensive Partnership and Cooperation Agreement	Vietnam
Partnership and Cooperation Agreement (PCA)	Iraq, Russia
Partnership Agreement	ACP
Cooperation Agreement	Syria
No agreement, Convention rates	China
No agreement, sanctioned	North Korea

It is important while reflecting on this to recall that the above list does not form a hierarchy of treaties. The reality is that any Venn diagram trying to place individual deals will end up looking like a map of the mediaeval Holy Roman Empire. Countries that are in a customs union, for example, are economically more integrated with the EU core than those in a Free Trade arrangement since border checks on goods have been removed; yet border checks on people may remain while a given counterpart has separately opted into the Schengen Zone allowing for passport-free entry for people. Meanwhile, the deals reached in two identical-sounding treaty types may be significantly different owing to such fundamental differences as the nature of the products exported from that part of the world, how far away it is (hence migration as an issue), or whether or not it's technologically developed or deals primarily in raw materials. The customs union involving San Marino understandably covers more items than Turkey's. Meanwhile, despite its treaty status, even Turkey has 17 FTAs of its own in force.[9]

What this list does by contrast confirm is that 'pick and mix' treaties are an accepted norm, as the EU reaches deals with its neighbours and even with its most insignificant trading partners. Malta prior to accession, for example, enjoyed an informal customs union for its exports while retaining tariff rights for the comparatively significant EU imports that came in. Or take the example of the Euro-Mediterranean Partnership. This divergent bloc of countries has total imports from the EU that are less than the amount that goes to the UK from the rest of the EU, of itself a pointer of the importance of the UK export market to other EU states. Within that partnership and just focusing on North Africa, the standard was originally a zero-rated import deal on basic goods which allowed for the counterpart Maghreb state to reduce annually by 10 per cent increments – in Algeria's case this was without that country even being a WTO member. The deal included preparation for further work on agricultural tariffs, the liberalisation of trade and investment, and agreements on accreditation and acceptance of industrial products. What followed starting with Tunisia was the rolling out of a DCFTA intended to 'extend significantly beyond the scope of the existing Association Agreement to include trade in services, government procurement, competition, intellectual property rights, and investment protection.' In other words, these are precisely the areas the UK is most interested in protecting its access rights to.

Geographically and simplistically put, the EU has focused on stabilisation-orientated trade deals in the Balkans; Partnership and Cooperation deals to the east; single market access to EFTA; customs union with Turkey and internal microstates; an Association Agreement with North Africa; advanced trade deals with NAFTA; FTAs with the emerging South Asian and Latin American markets; basic trade deals with developing countries; and attempted FTAs with the other distant but important markets. It is a truly complex jigsaw.[10]

That appears to leave the UK with a natural choice. Does it see itself as a rim state fitting into an EEA orbit; or an Anglo-Saxon world economy hotwired in through a super-FTA? The way the EU is globally orientated demonstrates that from its geographical preferences, the Commission is already pre-disposed to viewing the UK as fitting into either of these two trading clusters if it doesn't fit in at the core.

Therefore the question is: if the UK doesn't necessarily even need to be in the single market, does the UK want to be in an Association Agreement with the EU (effectively, a DCFTA) or just an FTA? If Algeria can get there, it seems all options are up for grabs.

But back to the published analysis. Comparing and contrasting the official gains made by shifting from one form of treaty to another, the author is able to suggest the existence of what he styles the *Freedom Curve*. Highly regulated countries that export a great deal to their EU counterparts will fare much better with increased integration into a highly regulated market. Those that are less so in either or both of those two areas will fare relatively, and after a certain point absolutely, worse.

Looking at the gains associated in cost-benefit accession papers, this generates three curves sketched out as follows:

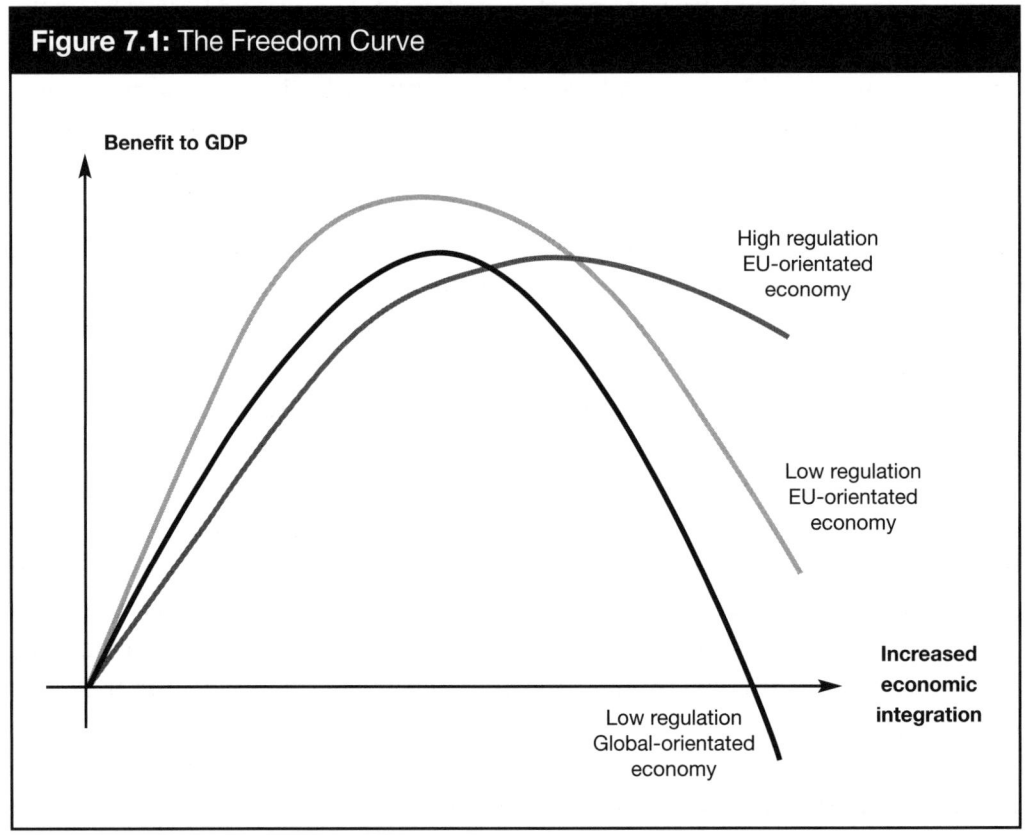

Figure 7.1: The Freedom Curve

Benefit to GDP

High regulation EU-orientated economy

Low regulation EU-orientated economy

Low regulation Global-orientated economy

Increased economic integration

Source: The Freedom Association, *Manning the Pumps*

As the author contends, the goal of the negotiators in our treaty talks is first to identify where on that black curve we find ourselves, as a lightly regulated economy with only a small share of our exports going to the EU. Looking back at the table showing the forms of association on offer, it suggests negotiating terms short of full membership by removing ourselves from a number of chapters of EU competences. That takes us into an orbit lying between types 4–7 on Table 7.3, or 3–7 if permitted EEA vetoes were actually used by the FCO.[11]

But again, for a full appreciation of the principles of the 'Goldilocks Zone' that are espoused, we commend the original paper for study in greater depth.[12]

(V) *Britain and Europe: A New Relationship*, by Dr Ruth Lea and Brian Binley, MP

Much of this report looks at the complex data surrounding the balance of interests around the UK's trading relationships. As a result it is a useful source of data, which understandably has also informed this book.

In sum, it suggests that Britain, under the WTO umbrella, should move towards the following trading relationships with EU and non-EU countries respectively. With EU countries: a Swiss-style relationship, based on free trade and mutually beneficial bilateral agreements; and with non-EU countries: closer trade links with the Commonwealth, the USA and other favoured nations. These links could include the establishment of a Commonwealth FTA and/or Britain's membership of NAFTA. NAFTA (North American Free Trade Agreement) could then become the North Atlantic Free Trade Agreement. By negotiating these closer relationships, Britain would be in a much better position to realign its trade patterns towards fast growing economies, thus stimulating economic growth, than it is now.

Building up mutually beneficial free trade links with the EU, Commonwealth and NAFTA would mean that, rather being isolated, Britain would actually be better internationally networked, especially with the world's growing economies, than as a member of the EU.

So in short, this would require getting a deal with the EU on terms of association that are limited to trade access rather than 'insider' EU membership.

(VI) *The Europe Report: A Win-Win Situation*, by Dr Gerard Lyons

Carrying a slightly stand-offish foreword from the Mayor of London who commissioned it, the Lyons Report nevertheless bears the imprimatur of the government entity responsible for standing up for the City. Its priorities include: halting the process of ever closer union; reforming the relationship between the Eurozone and non-Eurozone; completing the single market; fixing sector-specific problems; fixing a number of non-sector-specific problems; and issues such as the legal supremacy of the UK courts with respect to the single market.

The implications – admitted – are that such reforms go beyond legislative tweaks and require architectural adjustment to the treaties, sufficient to mean that the UK 'leaves' the EU as we currently see it without actually 'leaving' (formally) the EU through triggering an Article 50 declaration. The author also indicates that full withdrawal and renegotiated terms that maintain high levels of engagement with the continent are a happier default than staying stuck in the rut of enduring and unhappy full membership.

(VII) The Brexit Competition

The IEA in 2014 ran an open competition based on a specific scenario. The starting premise ran as follows:

> A referendum has resulted in an 'Out' vote and Her Majesty's Government has triggered Article 50 of the Lisbon Treaty. What measures does the UK need to take in the following two years, domestically (within the UK), vis-a-vis the remaining EU and internationally, in order to promote a free and prosperous economy?

From our vantage point in this paper, this is rather ahead of the game since we are looking at the terms of the treaty to be reached before the referendum itself. However, the principle does allow us to consider wider questions over what areas the UK would seek to reassociate itself with the core EU, and thus by extension before then we can extrapolate what our negotiating focus needs to be.

The Brexit prize winner was a paper by Iain Mansfield, *A Blueprint for Britain: Openness Not Isolation*. It proposes a system in which the UK is a member of EFTA but not the EEA, is outside the customs union, has free movement of goods, probably does not have free movement of agricultural goods, partial free movement in services and rescinded in people, free movement in capital, and a limited *acquis*. The critical paragraphs here run as follows:

> The UK will, inevitably, need to accept some EU regulation in order to gain the necessary trade access in both goods and services. Financial services are a particularly critical sector: from 2019 onwards, providers outside the EEA will only be able to offer a more limited range of services, unless they establish a subsidiary within the EEA13. In addition to the impact on UK businesses, London currently benefits as the subsidiary location of choice for financial companies from countries outside the EEA such as the USA and Switzerland. The UK should therefore seek to negotiate an exit agreement that will allow this access to be preserved, potentially accepting a certain degree of regulatory cooperation as the price for access.

> The UK should also be prepared to accept regulation on standards for electronic machinery or for health and safety inspection requirements for food exports: many of these will be based on international standards and similar in type if not specifics, to what exporters to other countries such as the US must abide by. There is no similar justification, however, once having left the EU[13], to accept regulation on purely internal matters such as working hours, hygiene requirements for domestic restaurants or mandatory quotas for women on boards.

This seems like a most basic baseline for what we should already be planning for our form of association from the outset, without having to lose a referendum first.[14] The only regulations that UK industry would actually need to implement would be the product regulations of the importing country, whether, say, the US, EU or China.

But perhaps more useful is another paper submitted to the competition by economist Philip Rush, later amended and published by Nomura Global Markets Research.[15] It proposes a more politically-acceptable alternative to the Swiss model by adopting a binary trading system, following EU rules when trading into the continent.

> The European Free Trade Area (EFTA) would remain an attractive grouping to join for its trade agreements. Between the set menu of the EEA and the pick-and-mix of the "Swiss option" is a simple association agreement that grants access to the single market and all its four freedoms. Of course, the chefs on the EU's negotiating team need an incentive to expand their menu. It is not feasible for them to allow unfettered competition from a potentially deregulated market. However, by forgoing the principle of origin for the UK services sector, UK firms would have to abide by EU rules when trading in the EU. The rest of the time they could stick to a potentially simpler UK system. EU firms would not have to face "unfair" competition from the UK but would still enjoy access to the UK market, appeasing them. And previous foreign establishments and migrants would not fall foul of legislative changes.

This model is not entirely dissimilar from that separately espoused by Business for Britain coming at it from the opposite direction.[16] In practical terms, Rush explains there would be three negotiating priorities:

> **1)** Access to the EU single market and its four freedoms would be crucial, including in labour, despite domestic political costs. Forgoing the principle of origin should allow agreement to be reached. This would spare most UK

output from EU rules, improving competitiveness with the world, but not the EU, making it agreeable to negotiators.

2) All freedoms must be legally enforceable to prevent them being flouted. Conceding jurisdiction in this area to the ECJ would make this clear, avoid disputes, fit with legal precedents and not require Treaty change. To enforce bounds in the agreement where intended, the UK may benefit from codifying its constitution and withdrawing from the Council of Europe, which could impose EU rules by the back door.

3) Maximising [these] gains would require deepening existing free trade agreements and striking new deals with other countries. Joining the European Free Trade Area would be a good start and would limit legal issues. Sending the right message is vital to limiting lost investment in the interim. Committing to cut taxes would demonstrate that the aim is essentially one of gaining from open competitiveness, not isolation.

There is nothing stopping FCO negotiators adopting these targets from the very outset as the objective framework for any new treaty.

(VIII) Lessons from Flexcit

One other Brexit entry deserves particular study. *Flexcit*, by Dr Richard North, may well as it progresses end up as the most comprehensive and considered review of how a post-Article 50 set of negotiations will need to look – at least until the FCO collectively gets into gear. This falls beyond our immediate scope in these pages.[17] But just as significantly, it is an important audit of how the UK mechanically in terms of its very governance is enmeshed in European and global systems of governance.

It usefully explores the actual back story of the decision making that led to the disastrous flooding of the Somerset Levels, a powerful case history in how EU-level decision making is cemented into the roots of UK governance and chokes localism. It investigates a number of intriguing and often-overlooked complexities and realities associated with the EEA, and covers a number of highly regulated areas (in particular, the environment, agriculture, and fisheries) where EU involvement is a huge burden.

Correspondingly, any attempt to shift from the current arrangements to any other arrangements need to reflect on how those strings are currently intertwined. It is correspondingly a technical must-read for Whitehall.

Renegotiation and models of association

> **Bottom lines up front**
> - Rather than aspire to marginally adjust the treaties (and dodge any referenda), planners need to look from scratch at what's wrong and seek to fix it through a new deal. Treaty of London, anyone?
> - Other countries are practically guaranteed to block this, though it is worth asking.
> - It shouldn't take more than a few days to find this out. But ambassadors need to be briefed that the policy is much more than cosmetic.
> - If the response is, as seems likely, negative we have to instantly shift from fixing the Treaty of Lisbon for everybody's benefit, to fixing just what's wrong with the Treaty of UK Accession.
> - That means understanding the EEA model properly, and starting to talk now about tariff-cutting deals if, after doing the maths, we decide to step outside the customs union entirely.

The task before our negotiators is therefore one of Gordian complexity and immense consequence. Properly grappled with, it is the mission of setting out an enduring generational association, creating a set of treaty terms that are wrought with sufficient strength to withstand the centralising trends inherent within the Brussels construct, yet allowing sufficient flexibility for our line to slacken if the Euro-core fish descends to the depths.

There will be a tendency in quarters of Whitehall to want to duck this challenge. Some will fall into the default of targeting a shallow, short-term solution. But there is today a rare prospect of achieving the objective of a settled and innovative shift.

It may well be that this cannot be done by modifying the text in the Treaty as it stands post-Lisbon. There will be strong voices raised against opening up clauses and pushing reform, just as 40 years ago the demand was on British politicians that they should swallow the basics whole.[18] Friends of the Commission will say that opening up any one aspect risks opening up others by other aggrieved parties – to which we can only say, good! The democratic deficit can only be reduced by doing this. Given the realities of world trade, we no longer see the disintegration of the single market being a realistic threat overhanging us. It is certainly a feeble excuse to prevent reform of the busted parts of the system (and it is also a hypocritical one, since conversely integrationists are quite happy to barter between them for extra powers to go the other way).

We do also accept that there will be many vested interests that will mobilise against significant changes to the treaties, stymie reform, and bruise the reformers. Our reforming friends in the Netherlands and elsewhere may not be enough to create a momentum for change. The realities will become very quickly apparent: it should swiftly become clear what the tidal range in the treaty text will be. If it proves Mediterranean rather than a Severn Bore, then we need to instantly move from a multilateral approach and take a bilateral one. We should accept that the Lisbon Plus world is not one we can change nor live within, then start to negotiate instead a bilateral treaty change that covers the UK's relationship.

Key to this is a paragraph that already lies within the EU treaty itself. Article 8, inserted by Lisbon, states:

> 1. The Union shall develop a special relationship with neighbouring countries, aiming to establish an area of prosperity and good neighbourliness, founded on the values of the Union and characterised by close and peaceful relations based on cooperation.
>
> 2. For the purposes of paragraph 1, the Union may conclude specific agreements with the countries concerned. These agreements may contain reciprocal rights and obligations as well as the possibility of undertaking activities jointly. Their implementation shall be the subject of periodic consultation.

This is as close as one can get to a formal invitation to readjust our treaties into a looser arrangement. Moreover, it is one which fits into current trends.

The current tendency is for partner countries to agree Deep and Comprehensive Free Trade Agreements (DCFTAs). These constitute far more than simple trade agreements, but fall short of full EU membership. A case in point is the one reached with the Ukraine and the cause of so much trouble with Russia. The EU-Ukraine DCFTA has a preamble designed to suit Ukrainian aspirations (of some small use in ECJ deliberations). Title I deals with general principles including democracy and basic freedoms. Title II covers domestic reform, and political and security cooperation. Title III covers a number of JHA aspects, including border controls. Title IV relates to trade. Title V goes over pretty much all the EU competences, and slots the Ukrainians into 28 chapters worth of arrangements short of EU membership. Title VI covers the money, and Title VII the institutions.[19]

The treaty runs to over 1,200 pages – about five times the size of the Lisbon Treaty. It consists of 486 articles and numerous annexes. It is a complex document – as the name suggests, it is both deep and comprehensive. But it falls short of conferring what we would understand as EU membership status.

It correspondingly proves the lie to any claim that the UK could not negotiate an all-encompassing deal that better suits the UK's purposes. This specific DCFTA (only one of several) is not in itself a precise text to aspire to. Ukraine politically has problems in aspiring to it itself. But the example does demonstrate the variety of models of association that the world of Article 8 now authorises.

Of course, our terms would be negotiated to suit *our* requirements and not Kiev's. Our deal would be designed not to harmonise with an objective of ultimate accession, but to define the limits of what needs to be harmonised at all. But equally, we would not be in the midst of an existential territorial dispute with a nuclear power while discussing them.

In a sense, the DCFTA model is not a recent invention. It is an alternate form to the trade association offered by the EEA model. This is a much-maligned and badly misunderstood model, as Table 7.5 shows. The reasons for maligning the model appear deliberate and strategic, in arguments put out by supporters of the status quo and continuing UK membership of the full-blown EU.

Table 7.5: EEA Model vs EU Model

Issue	EU Member	EEA Member
Amount of *acquis*	100 per cent	Just single market (8-19 per cent[20])
Judicial oversight	ECJ	'EEA Court', and just on single market
Veto	QMV the norm	Veto retained as applies to the UK
Parliamentary red card	None	Yes
MEPs' influence	Nationally fractional	Not needed (see above)
Budgetary contribution	Massive	Small and only thanks to a pro-EU government cave in
Influence legislation during drafting	Yes	Yes
Influence treaties during drafting by international bodies	No, where competence surrendered: Commission lead	Yes – usually veto

Central is the fact that EEA members only have to concern themselves with laws that relate to the single market. Already by 1992, the difference between the EEA *acquis* at around 13,000 pages and the Communities *acquis* around 95,000 pages was massive. The expansion of EU competences beyond trade concerns suggests that this gap has grown in the two decades since. That has obvious implications on red tape generation.

So the volume of rules is far smaller for EEA members. What about the way they are made? While Norway is sometimes described as a 'fax democracy' supposedly accepting rules sent from Brussels without any power to stop them, in reality this is utterly incorrect. EEA member states have the power of veto over any EU legislation that crosses their path. The fallacy perhaps in part arises rather because Oslo for a number of years has had governments that aspire to full EU membership and are very pro-Brussels, and so have declined to use the veto (much to the occasional anger of their counterparts in tiny Iceland, who have felt too isolated and small to kick up any fuss on their own).

That tide is now ebbing, and we are seeing Reykjavik, Oslo and Tórshavn (the Faroes has its own separate FTA) increasingly prepared to stand up for their rights under their agreements with the EU. There is no reason why the UK could not follow the same principles. Indeed, the threat of EU and EEA trade rules diverging would act as a spur to ensuring EEA members were fully happy with any new rules from the outset.

Other publications usefully expand further on why the Norway model is far more viable than opposing supporters of EU integration give credit for. Suffice it here to state that more honesty in that particular debate is called for. We recommend the references listed below for further review.[21] The key point we make once again is that 'stripped' models of association are perfectly legitimate ways of doing business.

It is not even as if the current model should just be left alone because we are doing well out of it. A damning study by Bertelsmann Stiftung in 2014 demonstrated that the integration associated with the direction of EU treaties suited certain core and Eurozone economies very well, but orbiting economies negligibly (see Figure 7.2).[22] Put simply, the treaties don't do 'outliers' with low levels of connectivity with the German economy any favours.[23]

Similar work recently undertaken for Civitas also directly challenges long-held assumptions about the value of our single market terms.[24] Its author writes, 'While the share of UK exports to fellow EU members has been virtually stable, the share going to non-members in Europe has risen steadily, leading one to suspect that both insider advantages and outsider disadvantages are imaginary.'

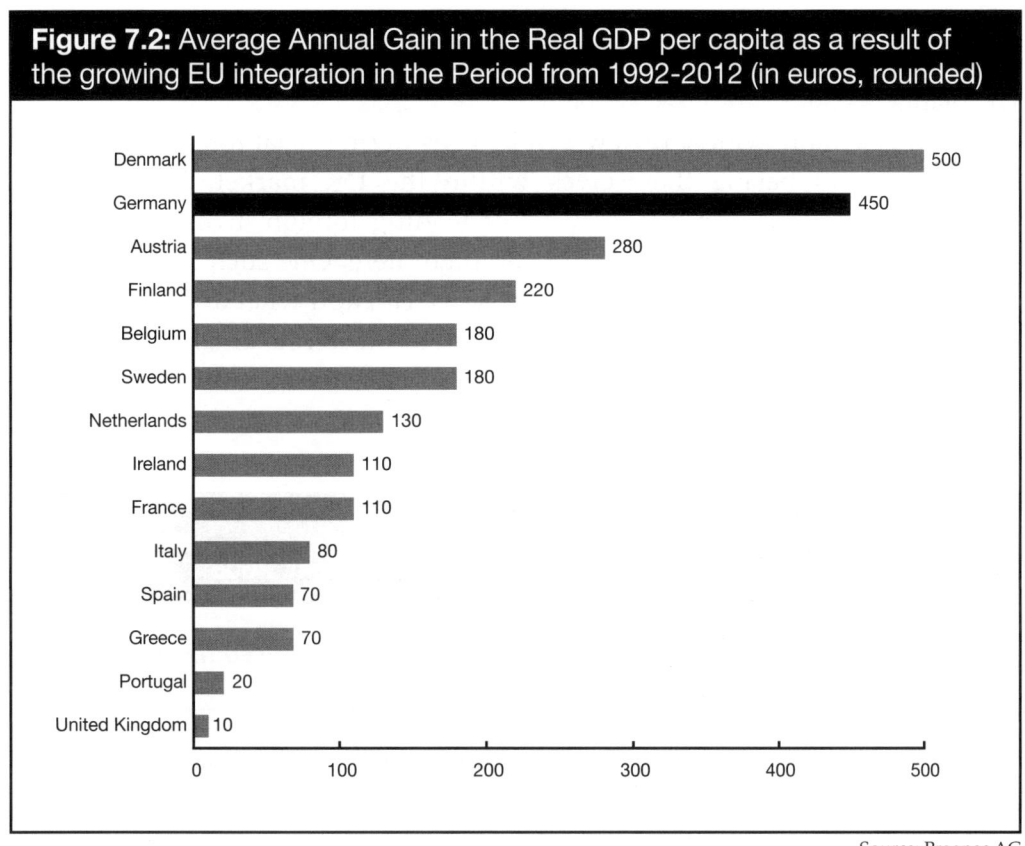

Figure 7.2: Average Annual Gain in the Real GDP per capita as a result of the growing EU integration in the Period from 1992-2012 (in euros, rounded)

Denmark	500
Germany	450
Austria	280
Finland	220
Belgium	180
Sweden	180
Netherlands	130
Ireland	110
France	110
Italy	80
Spain	70
Greece	70
Portugal	20
United Kingdom	10

Source: Prognos AG

He continues, 'Thus far, the single market has not enabled UK exports of goods or services to other members to grow at a faster rate than those of non-member exporters, nor at a faster rate than UK exports to non-member markets. It has been an era of decline for UK exporters, relative to both non-members in the same market, and to UK exports to other markets.'

If that is not an incentive to revisit our terms of access to the EU market, nothing is.

Some might challenge the impact this could have on Foreign Direct Investment (FDI), of which the UK is one of the EU's consistent top three recipients. Work by Ian Milne and Natalie Hamill on the key area of the UK's car industry has demonstrated that this is a bugbear of a defence.[25] Even during any period before a new FTA was negotiated, the removal of single market regulations – which are driving even French car manufacturers out of France – would counter much of the new tariff cost associated with being outside the Common External Tariff (CET) boundary. Furthermore, any attempt to hike tariffs would be reciprocated and damage the very significant (and powerful) continental vehicle manufacturing lobbies. Many of those incidentally also have major interests in UK plants.

We can also more widely review FDI by considering what foreign businesses like best about basing themselves within the UK market. Business and government on occasion run surveys of leading foreign investors on what brought them to the UK and might keep them here. One such compilation in 2008 identified 20 key attractions. To these we can add what aspects might be under threat from a significant renegotiation of our terms of association with the EU; and what are under threat from failing to negotiate anything at all. These are set out in Table 7.6 below.

Table 7.6: Top 20 reasons to do business in the UK: *Investing in the UK*, UK Trade and Investment, 2008

Reason given for investment	Dependent on EU membership?	EU Threat
The easiest place to set up and run a business in Europe: The World Bank found that it takes 13 days to set up a business in the UK, compared to the European average of 32 days. It ranked the UK first in Europe and sixth in the world to operate a business. Source: World Bank.	No – a consequence of 1980s domestic reform.	High: social chapter threats to start ups.
Low tax rate environment for foreign investors: The top corporate rate has dropped below most of the UK's core competitors. The UK has reduced its corporate tax rate from over 50 per cent in the early 1980s down to one of the lowest in the industrialised world. The UK's highest personal tax band is one of the lowest in the EU. Source: Forbes Tax Misery Index.	No – dependent on domestic policy.	High: Commission is currently reviewing Irish Corporation Tax levels for example on 'level playing field' principles.
One of the most flexible labour markets in Europe: The World Bank ranked the UK the second best place in Europe to employ workers, just behind Denmark. Source: World Bank.	No – indeed, the Anglo-Dutch model contrasts with the Rhineland model pushed at Brussels.	Very high: considerable and ranging social chapter threats.
Least barriers to entrepreneurship in the world: The OECD noted that the UK was second in the world for Product Market Regulation behind Australia, had the least barriers to entrepreneurship in the world and had the third lowest barriers to trade and investment in the world. Source: OECD.	No – regulation actually augmented by single market obligations.	Varying: reduced barriers internal to the single market at cost of higher global barriers, plus significant regulatory burdens across both.

Reason given for investment	Dependent on EU membership?	EU Threat
World leader in innovation: The UK was one of the most productive places for innovation firms in the world ranking second only to the USA for the quality of its research base.	Partial. Some issues potentially over receipt of EU research grants, but these are divvied up across participating states including non-EU countries, are dependent on research quality, and the UK is a net budget contributor anyway.	Uncertain: centralising tendencies exist over patenting, endorsing defensive patenting practices for large corporations to threaten mutual litigation wars.
One of the most stable political environments to do business: According to Transparency International, the UK was one of the most transparent (least corrupt) countries in the world. It had a higher rating than France, Germany, USA and Japan.	No – the UK is a driver of good governance/ transparency in the EU.	High: EU budgetary fraud and incentives to dodge bad laws (e.g. 'black fish' CFP quota surplus) part of business reality.
Booming economy: The UK has one of the highest GDP growth rates in Europe, well above the European and Eurozone averages. Source: OECD.	No – outside of Eurozone, running Atlantic rather than Rhineland economic cycles.	Very high: high regulatory impact coupled with Eurozone dangers threaten long term stability.
One of the easiest countries to register a property: to register a property, the UK was ranked above France, Germany, Ireland and Italy. Source: Cushman and Wakefield.	No (there are five different methods used across the EU – and France and Italy even have different systems in territories gained in 1919)	Uncertain: legislation targeting money laundering may generate a complex costly assets register.
Commitment to improving the planning regime: The recent Energy White Paper by the Department of Business, and the government-commissioned Barker 2 Review of Land-use Planning and Economic Development, outline speedier planning consents for business.	No.	Significant: EU Environmental Impact Assessments, based on an array on eco-directives.
Speaking in the international language of business: Operating in English gives firms in the UK a natural advantage when communicating globally.	No.	None.
Progressive communications network: The UK has the most extensive broadband market among the G7 countries and one of the strongest ICT infrastructures in the world.	Unlikely: mobile roaming changes unlikely to be reversed.	May generate significant long term burdens owing to human rights obligations.
Extant business position: London is the world's leading financial services centre on a number of key performance indicators and was voted top European city for business for the 17th year running in 2006 by the European Cities Monitor.	Uncertain. City faces Eurozone competition which might get more bitterly contested outside of EU. This is likely to happen anyhow.	Considerable: Frankfurt is sold as the premier Euro-zone economic centre, and home to the ECB. Paris sees strategic advantage in damaging the City. The UK's global context and opportunities are hampered by EU regulation.

Reason given for investment	Dependent on EU membership?	EU Threat
Top talent: The UK has the top six universities in Europe and two of the top three globally. Source: *Times Higher Education Supplement*.	No.	Indirect: harmonisation of access rights (viz English students in Scotland).
Springboard to Europe: The UK provides direct access to the single market and is geographically on the continent of Europe.	Yes, at least for the former... But trade access not necessarily dependent on EU membership.	No (provided that UK accepts costs and damages that go with it, which is precisely the problem).
Number of European headquarters: More overseas companies have set up their European headquarters in the UK than anywhere else.	Uncertain and dependent upon the balance of other benefits.	Variable: regulations may attempt to draw HQs into the Eurozone, or just make the UK unattractive and drive outside of UK/EU entirely. But consider how well Switzerland fares in comparison!
Olympic opportunities: contract opportunities existed for billions of pounds. (- No longer relevant -)	No	A case study found the UK advertising job opportunities across the EU far more than other countries. In 2013, over half of EURES-listed jobs were in the UK, three times Germany's adverts, and seven thousand times Poland's.
Transport links: The UK offers a world-class transport network offering rapid links to mainland Europe and the rest of the world. Heathrow is Europe's largest air hub, with on-going expansions improving its efficiency. London boasts one of the world's largest over ground and underground rail networks.	Mixed. TENs grants to the UK are disproportionately low and could be generated by national government. Single Skies/aviation agreements unlikely to fall apart given aerospace realities. Airline slots would need settling, but Heathrow and Gatwick are huge bartering chips.	Significant. EU policy cost impacts disproportionately owing to fewer cross-border benefits – e.g. privatisation model of rail track; weight limits per axle on lorries.
High quality of living: UK residents enjoy a high standard of living, education and recreation. Personal taxes are low, publicly-funded health is free to all and there is a rich cultural heritage and abundance of leisure facilities	No	Significant and multiple risks. For instance: tax harmonisation; ECJ risks to independent NHS management; impact of immigration demographics on quality of life, e.g. population-driven housing bubble and demand on amenities.
Magnet for foreign investment: In 2006, the UK attracted and retained over $1tn of investment, the highest in Europe and the second largest in the world.	Mixed. Some transient FDI uncertainty in some sectors but none in others, plus red tape gains.	High (see rest of table!)

Reason given for investment	Dependent on EU membership?	EU Threat
Productivity rapidly increasing: Historically, the UK had lower productivity than its main competitors, but this is changing and the UK has closed the gap somewhat.	No.	High owing to EU welfare costs.

[First column paraphrased for brevity, columns 2 and 3 our analysis]

From that list we can see that the reasons listed by British businesses themselves for attracting FDI are extremely varied and very little to do with EU membership. It is true that it does feature as one of a handful of significant considerations. Nevertheless, reaching a treaty settlement that facilitates continuing access to the continental export markets would result in a list that pretty well matches the one given above, but with the additional bonus of removing some of the burdens of regulation.

The dangerous element is what lies in the third column. Not instigating any change in the way we do business with the single market puts our appeal to investors very much in jeopardy over the long term.

Strategically, it is imperative that we reshape our trading terms with the EU. We have to recreate our treaty in a most fundamental way. If all of the EU will not reform to create a light-touch EU, as seems sadly predestined, we must shift our negotiating stance to one of reformulating our association to remove ourselves to a gentler orbit around this constraining mass.

Where now?

Bottom lines up front

- The red lines have to allow continuing trade access but maximise the opportunity to ditch unnecessary red tape – and there is a lot of it.
- The Commission prefers uniformity; but the other member states who actually sign the treaties will realistically want their exports to continue. A deal is achievable.
- The end result ultimately will be a model that's not full EU membership. Nor will it be Norwegian, Swiss, Turkish, DCFTA, CEFTA, TTIP, FTA, GSP, MFN, nor indeed the myriad of other EU treaty terms already today on offer.

- Something can be tailored that's mutually suited for the trading that happens between the UK and the EU: a Channel Treaty.
- The central variable is the Treasury's own assessment of what deals can be done over tariffs.

Table 7.7: Treaty Chapters – What EU Competences are Superfluous from a UK Perspective

Type	Solution	Competence Field
Cat A	Remove and deal with nation states on a UK-country bilateral basis	Chapter 11: Agriculture and rural development Chapter 13: Fisheries Chapter 17: Economic and monetary policy Chapter 19: Social policy and employment Chapter 20: Enterprise and industrial policy Chapter 22: Regional policy Chapter 26: Culture Chapter 31: Foreign, security and defence policy
Cat B	Remove and replace with UK-EU bilaterals on a case-by-case basis	Chapter 2: Free movement of workers Chapter 3: Right of establishment Chapter 9: Financial services Chapter 10: Information society and media Chapter 12: Food safety Chapter 14: Transport policy Chapter 15: Energy Chapter 16: Taxation Chapter 21: Trans-European networks Chapter 23: Judiciary and fundamental rights Chapter 24: Justice, freedom and security Chapter 27: Environment Chapter 34: Institutions
Cat C	Keep while renegotiation is ongoing; public debate; and official audit	Chapter 1: Free movement of goods Chapter 4: Free movement of capital Chapter 8: Competition policy Chapter 29: Customs union Chapter 33: Financial and budgetary provisions Chapter 35: Other issues[26]
Cat D	Keep within the UK-EU treaty	Chapter 3: Freedom to supply services Chapter 5: Public procurement Chapter 6: Company law Chapter 7: Intellectual property law Chapter 18: Statistics Chapter 25: Science and research Chapter 26 Education (year abroad only) Chapter 28: Consumer and health protection Chapter 30: External relations Chapter 32: Financial control

The reader will by now be aware that our red line strokes have been undertaken with a roller brush. A finer appreciation has to be drawn by the negotiators from a confederacy of artists with sketches covering a multitude of subjects, some of whom we listed as our 'Magic Eight'.

Yet we may still profitably here reflect on which specific pillars of the treaties we must remove, to enhance the global vistas from our porch.

Table 7.7, above, lists the 35 chapters into which accession negotiations are divided for countries seeking to join the EU. It appears to make just as much sense to consider each now, as we reflect on our remeasured treaty status heading in the other general direction.

These are broken down into four headings, depending on where what is currently done in Brussels might best be agreed in the future. It is, of course, subjective.

Category A comprises our suggestion of items that have no place in the communal Brussels treaties. Including any item from this category into an EU treaty is an encouragement and an endorsement to creating a federal superstate, so these powers need to be removed. In areas where cooperation is required, this can be achieved by joint action, either bilaterally or multilaterally but outside of the EU structures. The CAP, as we have seen, is a prime example. Removing it from the terms of the UK's treaty instantly means the UK no longer is a formal EU member, nor even an EEC-style member. The policy is, however, a huge drain on consumers and taxpayers, and a block on our traditional Commonwealth links. Running it as an independent policy provides us with a powerful lever in negotiating other association elements with countries such as France, and allows for a national debate on how best to manage and subsidise our agrarian industry and rural environment. The CFP for its part should never have been communitarised in the first place, and the manner in which this was achieved was both immoral and technically (for all that is worth) illegal under EEC law.

Since we are admitting we are never joining the euro, Chapter 17 no longer applies. Social policy and Chapter 19 need to be stripped entirely from the EU relationship. This removes the waste associated with the European Social Fund as well as the burdens of excessive health and safety. The Labour Party and others may well cherish the social chapter, but it's based on an original Social Charter by the Council of Europe, and any future Labour government is quite able to introduce into UK domestic law any measures that it pleases in any event. Doing so under a national authority rather than a transnational one allows bad laws to be repealed or amended after parliamentary debate, which cannot happen under the current system.[27] Chapter 20, enterprise and industrial policy, is largely an excuse for the Commission to back corporations and select 'winners'. Regional policy and Chapter 22 is largely an excuse to claw back some EU funds, and subsidiarity here can flow directly downwards from the national capital as the originating peak.

Chapter 26 is often used as an excuse to subsidise the development of an 'EU demos', since young people are seen as key and particularly vulnerable 'opinion multipliers'. One aspect of this area which could usefully be retained is the academic exchange programme for students, facilitating the Erasmus Programme. The logic behind the funding for Jean Monnet programmes by contrast is highly contentious.

Foreign, security and defence policy under Chapter 31 would also be shifted. Rather than simply defaulting back to its original second pillar location, a more meaningful solution would be to prioritise cooperation with effective deploying states. This in particular means the French.[28] The medium of preference would remain NATO, with all its added potential.[29]

The UK's direct participation in the institutions such as the European Parliament under Chapter 34 no longer make sense if the treaty is stripped down.[30] Assuming major changes are indeed made to the UK treaty, then UKREP's offices would move, and UK nationals would be phased out of the Commission.[31] It need not be a major concern. Other trading partners of the EU manage with far less. However, greater emphasis could be placed on the link office run by parliament at the EP in spotting issues that might be of concern by the other, arising at EEA conclaves. Currently it's a small scale effort but it could become a key resource.

Secondly, under **Category B**, there are those areas we might choose to remove from our EU treaty arrangements, which will remain a central competence for the EU, and where we generate bilaterals on a case-by-case basis with the EU as the collective negotiating partner. Consequently, in drafting successor agreements on the free movement of workers and the right of establishment with those countries where the UK has the greatest interest (Spain, Ireland, France), EU norms will increasingly apply and it might be more satisfactory to work out new terms at Brussels. Given the desire to introduce a managed system more closely dependent on actual economic need, this means disapplying the current permissive freedom of movement for the workforce (as opposed to workers) and reapplying a measure of oversight that simply wasn't required when the concept was originally introduced.[32] Naturally, agreements will have to be in place to provide mutual structures, for instance for managing social security cover: this does not, however, necessarily need to be uniform across the EU, or unilaterally generous by either party.

Financial services need a firewall to keep the ECJ at bay: that means separate bilateral arrangements covering the City and its Eurozone counterparts. It may be that this closely resembles much of what is already in existence, at least in terms of oversight; the merits of other *acquis* might be individually tested against the burdens faced by New York rather than Frankfurt. We acknowledge that City access to the Eurozone markets would need to be linked to other trade access areas. Indeed, protecting the City's interests and the mirrored needs of the continent in financially accessing its resources guarantees that any new UK-EU treaty would be, and would need to be, *sui generis*.

The horse lasagne scandal demonstrated that the food safety system can no longer be unilaterally trusted at EU level, though Chapter 12 cooperation with the single market could cautiously be managed at Brussels. Taxation and Chapter 16 issues need to be through unanimity, focusing just on avoiding subsidy. Looser affiliation here means potential for a hugely reduced set of 'membership fees'. We also regain control over cutting or zero-rating VAT rates. Sticking with the single market option during renegotiation instead means having to maintain this as an EU competence.

Chapter 14 covers transport policy. As we do not have canals or motorways readily passing from one border to the next, this might usefully be left to deal with bilaterally. This would also excuse us the cost of vastly subsidising the other transit nations under Chapter 21. Aviation will need some work on it, so that the UK should be expected to maintain grandfather rights and obligations in bilaterals covering such issues as slots, access and mutual recognition of standards. Given the growing interdependence of the continental grid, we might expect the EU to be the logical partner for discussing energy cooperation, though bilaterals with the French may in particular be sought. This requires the ECJ to keep out of UK North Sea interests, and the Commission to separate environmental and supply concerns, so major elements are best done bilaterally rather than through a common policy structure.

If we are repatriating the ECHR, then Chapter 23 with judiciary and fundamental rights has no place in a basic EU treaty either. Parliament can approve on a case-by-case basis whether it wants the EAW, and can leave its application to the domestic courts to arbitrate. That means also Chapter 24 and justice, freedom and security, which used to be a separate 'pillar' of the treaties lying outside the EU, needs to be put into a far more distinct and more readily modifiable condition. This also has direct bearing on border controls. In some areas, reasonable arguments can be made for international cooperation on a continental footing, and the EU may be a logical partner in data sharing in particular.

Environmental decisions should be returned to national control under Chapter 27, particularly the power for diplomats to make their own deals. In practice this would also need a revolution within DEC to prevent the department's eco-kamikaze delegates actively pushing economically illiterate drafts.

Then there are the areas (**Category C**) where the UK might currently park an end decision on a complex issue. Adherence to EU norms would continue for a transitional period. This would allow time for a proper official audit, and a public debate on the back of it. This is particularly true of Chapter 1, the free movement of goods. In short, the fundamental question is whether it is economically in the UK's national interest to pay red tape costs while remaining within the customs union, or instead seek bilateral terms by trading in from outside it. The answer to this depends in large part on whether Whitehall's analysis is that the Commission is genuine in currently seeking to shift its emphasis from product specifications to product requirements – in other words, whether it likes putting out precise and complex regulations on what products should look like, or much more effectively the rules on what products should do (or indeed not do, like melt or poison or break).

Global trade agreements are generally modelled on the latter approach, which is why being outside the customs union could cut red tape costs for UK businesses and make them more competitive. But this is also predicated upon Whitehall and politicians of all parties being inclined to take the opportunity to dump all the *acquis* that burdens the economy and is no longer legally required, certainly as far as the overwhelming majority of trade that doesn't get exported into the single market is concerned.

So there are fundamental variables at stake here. The end decision needs to be based on how determined a government will be to make the most of the opportunity. If the sense is that there is no appetite for a bonfire of red tape, then it would be a tragedy, but it may then make more sense to aim for a trade deal that keeps us within an EEA setting. By contrast, an ambitious government that seeks to make us globally competitive would instead be cause for negotiations to focus on cutting tariffs from outside the customs union. These talks could possibly take time, suggesting that the best parking space is transitionally also within the EEA while these tariff deals are being made.

If the objective was confirmed as moving beyond the single market, a major element of this would review how to cover the process of CE marking and conformity notifications. To a significant extent this would be mitigated by agreed trading standards. For example, 80 per cent of the Electromagnetic Capability Directive, 2004/108/EC, was lifted straight from IEC standards and just given European EN prefixes. However, testing and certification mechanisms would need to be confirmed for products based on, for instance, IEC rather than EU electromagnetic norms, in such a way not to pointlessly burden businesses. In reality this is no different from standard international trade management.

We are optimistic that the UK does not need to stick with an EEA arrangement and can seek better terms outside the customs union. As we saw earlier, the volume of our EU exports as compared with our internal and non-EU trade means that single market red tape costs may well already exceed the increased trade arising from single market access. If negotiators can cut the red tape costs without increasing product conformity or tariff costs commensurately, moving outside the customs union (i.e. the whole EEC infrastructure) makes perfect sense.[33]

Further official study is also needed on what EU tariffs we may genuinely expect to be reimposed under the various options, which countries are likely to intervene to protect their own key exports and block this, what subsidies might assist in transition, what could be offset by sectorial and tax gains from counter tariffs levied on EU imports, what domestic markets would open up in response, and which alternative foreign markets might increasingly prove attractive destinations.

Since joining the EEC, subsequent world trade agreements have cut global tariff levels so that if the UK does now exit the customs union and has to rely on the default external standard rates run by the EU, at 5.19 per cent simple average bound rates they are half of what encouraged the UK to join the EEC on economic grounds in the first place. A number of course run lower than this average: petroleum at 2.05 per cent, non-electrical machinery at 1.73 per cent, electrical machinery at 2.45 per cent. Particular focus would immediately by contrast need to be given to tariffs as applied to beverages (21.19 per cent – an obvious concern to the whisky industry, though the UK is also a major importer of EU wares, and currently-high domestic tax rates could be cut to compensate) and also clothing (11.51 per cent, though the UK is also a significant EU importer).

That means that there are three key areas where EU average tariffs currently run at over 4 per cent, generating a major mark up for the UK if any tariff deal was not found – food/drink/tobacco; clothing and footwear; and cars. Since

Spain alone exported €740m in fruit to the UK in 2013, France €1.3bn in wine, Italy €500m in shoes, and Germany €16bn in cars, we might predict some space for latitude from our trading partners.

But let's take the worst case scenario. The UK in 2012 had an economy estimated at £1,562bn – a trillion and a half. £52.2bn of UK exports to the EU are at risk of becoming subject to significant tariffs, amounting to 38.7 per cent of all EU exports. Consequently, 3.3 per cent of GDP is behind the drive for the UK to remain within the customs union. However, the actual costs of the tariffs that would be levied would amount, again at a worst case scenario, to £2.55bn, meaning the equivalent of 0.15 per cent of the UK economy. This, it turns out, is less than the rounding error for the rounding error that's known as the Rotterdam/Antwerp effect (the trade that gets masked as it's exported globally via one of these EU ports). That's well under half of the additional red tape costs Business for Britain estimates have accrued to British businesses from the Lisbon Treaty (£6bn). So we need to put these tariffs, significant though they are, into their fuller context.[34]

In other words, we might expect German car manufacturers to lobby to prevent EU-UK vehicle tariffs being imposed, and French farmers going on the streets the moment they fear their cheese and wine getting hit by the very significant rates that international trade rules allow. The economic shift generates tariff questions; political reality provides opportunities; both generate reasonable questions that should be far from insurmountable and appear to be economically advantageous. But government needs to be doing serious economic audits of it so that the sums and assumptions are in the public domain.[35] This in turn sets the terms over Chapter 29 and the nature of the UK's access to the customs union, as well as how EU funds are levied under Chapter 33.

Competition policy raises some fundamental questions. Keeping it as an EU competence effectively confirms the UK is in a single market agreement with the ECJ as a trade arbiter. But other models do exist, and the EEA members signally elected to set up a distinct trade court separate from that of Luxembourg. It is a court we might usefully consider the possibility of attaching ourselves to.

The final **Category, D**, is a list of those areas in which we see there being scope for continued activity with the EU as a continental forum. There is a case to be made for the mutual recognition of qualifications to fall within this area. The same is true of the application of rules governing services under Chapter 3, since this has been an area under tardy development for the last 20 years. This delay of itself suggests inherent logjams in liberalising an area of particular UK trade benefit. Reaching agreements about the free movement of capital for its part might perhaps be kept at Brussels, though there are obvious concerns about the threat to the City from policing this. So some measure of distance between the City and Brussels regulators needs to be generated, especially in advance of the Eurozone becoming their key priority. Public procurement (Chapter 5) could still be carried out under open competition systems, though only if international open competition and advertising starts to be taken seriously by other countries and the 2014 EU Procurement Directives begin to demonstrably work.

It appears to make sense to stick with a common system of working out comparable statistics (Chapter 18), especially after – and notwithstanding – the November 2014 EU surcharge fiasco. Science and research meanwhile (Chapter 25) might be managed through set treaty terms as these less obviously impinge on democratic accountability, and the UK is a prominent co-operator in a number of projects which in any case often transcend EU or even EEA borders. We might also concede Chapter 28 on consumer protection lends itself to common standards on policing the market place, though we would have to find a mechanism to ensure that the precautionary principle did not dominate processes.

Chapter 30 covers external relations, and member states adhering to EU treaties with third parties where Brussels has reached an agreement on a delegated power. Naturally, the UK would need to retain this commitment, though the actual list of agreements covered would be reduced in tandem with the competences list. Under the principle of *pacta sunt servanda*, the UK would be expected to honour existing commitments with third parties while assuming direct responsibility for renegotiating or abrogating them over time.[36] That includes of course the prospect of further extending them to suit particular UK interests, capabilities, and focus.

Chapter 32 covers avoiding fraud in EU grants so would stay, though without the threat of a European FBI being given powers down the line to track it, which is an ongoing aspiration.

Listing in Category C or D does not mean to say that there are no flaws in the way these issues have been run, nor indeed directives that could be usefully repealed. It is a strategic suggestion on how to manage international agreements at a European level in the future.

These are interpretations that are open to discussion; that should be discussed; that in Whitehall are not being discussed. Indeed, it seems that with the passage of four decades since the UK left EFTA, there is absolutely no memory in Whitehall of such a fundamental strategic debate at all.[37]

Overall, a lot of the EU treaties can be stripped away. It makes sense to aim for a bespoke deal covering just the trade and allowing cooperation in areas where we have a communal interest, but without surrendering our veto or letting the ECJ judges subjectively interpret the legislation.

Since we are unlikely to fix the Treaty of Lisbon, and can't go back to the Treaty of Rome, we will ultimately need to go beyond the 1972 Treaty of Brussels and sign a new Treaty of London. Then the Eurozone countries can continue to integrate as they realise what a botched decision they've made, but henceforth without blaming us.

As it happens, what we suggest is an optimal end result is not a million miles away from what several countries have already been able to achieve: a bit less than EEA terms, a bit more than DCFTA terms.

Everything depends on the likely achievable deals over the tariffs, that is to say what we can achieve beyond the already significantly lowered standard WTO rates that would automatically kick in – and for that we need the input from the Treasury.

Conclusion

> **Bottom lines up front**
>
> - All parties should aim to fix the UK's misaligned relationship with the EU. Other political bodies will be developing and setting out their own aspirations.
> - The single market has its costs and should be neither taboo nor sacrosanct as a subject.
> - Many other forms of trade treaty access apply between the EU and third parties. 100 per cent EU programme participation is simply not the only show in town.
> - Before the UK starts negotiating, it needs to define its red lines. Before it can sensibly do that, it needs to run a comprehensive and fair cost-benefit analysis of the current (and prospective) EU terms. Otherwise we are grappling in the dark.

Looking at how the EU works, we can begin to identify those parts of the machinery of governance where a number of key cogs are badly worn and essential bits of wiring are dangerously exposed.

The intent of half of the current coalition is to fix it. From our review, we suggest that changes may well prudently focus on: the sovereignty and accountability deficit; a holistic set of policies on the migrant-addicted economy; bullet-proofing the City; plugging the rebate, waste, and Eurozone drag; reconfiguring access to global markets, understanding the costs that go with the 'single market' or customs union; and localism as a motor for repatriating powers best removed from Brussels.

But that is not a prescriptive list. This paper does not set out a full list of the minimum terms that need to be won. We have just selected key ones as a starting point for the debate.

It's certainly critically important that as we have this debate, we are honest about what various treaty obligations mean. When we talk about wanting to have access to the single market, that can mean either being able to trade into it from outside but while facing extra tariffs in certain, finite, areas; or it can mean sitting within it but with some ongoing tensions, perhaps including free movement of workers and attempts to elasticate social rights as business commitments.

We deserve to have that debate. The best way of doing that is to go back to basics, and figure out what we *do* want from the EU as much as what we *don't*. That means looking at the future talks from the perspective of a single treaty construct with bolt-ons, rather than trying to peel away layers of the onion and just ending up crying.

The single market has gained a mystical and hallowed aura. Perhaps this was merited when it was first set up a generation of politicians ago, but world trade has moved on. So too, sadly, has the EC that the single market fostered. It is now the EU with all the costly additional appliances that Maastricht, Nice and Lisbon have subsequently added. The balance of benefit previously associated with this trading bloc has been eroded. We need to do the sums rationally and dispassionately on how we do trade into it.

The EU's array of third party trading agreements show that other viable options do exist. The DCFTA with the Ukraine and other states east of the Carpathians is just one proof of many. The recent EU-South Korean trade treaty shows that complex agreements can be reached, given the time and the inclination, allowing for business without membership but giving scope for cooperation in areas of mutual advantage. The deal with Seoul, incidentally, runs to a fairly comprehensive 1,338 pages. About 95 per cent of this is made up of technical lists. It sets out to 'progressively and reciprocally' liberalise trade in goods and services. It's governed by an arbitration panel, reaching their decisions ideally but not necessarily by consensus. Their rulings are meant to be complied with in good faith, but they do not generate legal obligations.

Alternatively, the reader may be interested in looking at the clauses that might be cut-and-paste from the EU-Chile Association Agreement; the EU-Mexico Economic Partnership, Political Cooperation and Cooperation [sic] Agreement; the EU-South Africa Trade, Development and Cooperation Agreement; the EU-Canada Comprehensive Economic and Trade Agreement; the EU-Gulf Cooperation Council Free Trade Agreement; the EU-India Free Trade Agreement; the EU-Malaysia Free Trade Agreement; the EU-Singapore Free Trade Agreement; the EU-Central America regional Association Agreement; the EU-Andean Community regional Association Agreement; or the EU-Mercosur regional

Association Agreement – to name just a few of the bloc bilaterals reached or in the process of being negotiated.[1]

From this increasing variety, we might readily conclude that a single blanket treaty that covers us in the same breath as all the other member states is, over the long term, not the best way forward. The world is gradually catching up with the EU in low tariff terms.[2] At some point, and we have in all likelihood already passed it, being a full EU member is too costly politically and economically for a country like the UK. We don't need the full gym membership.

The cost-effective route is then one of separate association treaties, with current key titles removed.

In effect, that takes us to being of the EU but not in the EU, rather like Churchill's way of looking at our relationship with the continent: associated, but not absorbed. It also starts to finally answer the old Dean Acheson conundrum about the role of the UK post-Empire, as the independent bridge between the continents on either side of the Atlantic.

Given that fact, new instructions should immediately be issued to those in Whitehall and especially to those who have been involved in the Balance of Competences Review. Led by the Treasury, they should now finally audit the actual costs of each of the treaty sections they have been looking into; and 11 Downing Street should then add up the sums as an adjunct to the final report.[3] other words, we need a genuine cost-benefit analysis and we need it quickly.[4]

We simply do not need to be in a treaty association that, like some crazy insurance plan, adds unnecessary costs to the deal we really need. We should go minimalist and lift out just the trade sections; and then on top of those aspects, individually add on those bits in which we think cooperation does work for us if we sit together in a room at Brussels working on them. Much of that will turn out best done bilaterally with individual member states.

Let us begin from the beginning. If we are to draw out red lines in our sea defences, psychologically we should start mapping from the low tide and plan upwards, rather than begin at the already-crumbling cliff edge.

So, what are the key minimum terms required to make our membership of the EU work? They are the requirements that need to be upheld by our negotiators. When it comes down to it, in reality it's just the two.

Honesty, and open-mindedness.

Appendices

APPENDIX A – Some Key ECJ Case Law Precedent Associated with Integration[1]

Judged	Case	Consequence
1963	Van Gend en Loos v Nederlandse Administratie der Belastingen (Case 26/62)	Customs rules in the treaties become directly effective.
1963	Da Costa en Schake N.V. v Nederlandse Belastagingenad-ministratie (Cases 28-30/62)	National courts should still send cases for review by the ECJ even if they judge case law is clear.
1963	Van Gend en Loos v Nederlandse Administratie der Belastinge (Case 26/62)	Direct effect and the supremacy of EC law over national law.
1964	Costa v ENEL (Case 6/64)	EC rights and duties limit sovereign rights, and cannot be unilaterally overridden by a national parliament. The ECJ must be appealed to for review of EC relevant cases even if national courts have no authority.
1969	Stauder v City of Ulm (Case 29/69)	Fundamental rights are recognised by EC law.
1970	Grad v Finanzamt Traunstein (Case 9/70)	Directives can be directly effective.
1970	Internationale Handelsgesellschaft mbH v Einfuhr-und Vor-ratsstelle fur Getreide und Futtermittel (Case 11/70)	The protection of fundamental rights, while inspired by the constitutional traditions common to the member states, must be ensured within the framework and structure of the objectives of the EC.

1971	Commission of the European Communities v. Council of the European Communities (Case 22/70)	Grant of internal competences gives the EEC external power as well (i.e. treaty-making prerogative).
1972	Sabbatini v EP (Case 20/71)	The Equal Treatment Directive should be interpreted liberally and should not be limited in scope to discrimination on grounds of gender.
1974	Transocean Marine Paint Association v EC Commission (Case 17/74)	A measure may be annulled where it is in breach of a general principle of EC law. That includes international law or domestic law.
1976	Defrenne v Sabena (Case 43/75)	Directives can create both horizontal and vertical effect, in an area of EC competence.[2] Defrenne cases mean gender equality provisions to gain direct effect.
1976	Procureur du Roi v Royer (Case 48/75)	State unable to ban undesirables entering their country to look for work or rejoin family.
1978	Italian Minister of Finance v Simmenthal (Case 106/77)	A national court should not apply conflicting national legislation nor wait for the decision of a higher national court before acting.
1979	Pubblico Ministero v Ratti (Case 148/78)	If no deadline is specified in a directive it takes effect on publication in the Official Journal.
1979	Commission v UK (Case 128/78)	Difficulty in implementing a bad law should not stop the law being implemented.
1980	Roquette Freres S.A. v Council (Case 138/79)	The European Parliament can use the ECJ to protect its treaty rights.
1982	Levin v Staatssecretaris van Justitie (Case 53/81)	Freedom of movement trumps national rights to require them to have a job.[3]
1983	Charmasson v. Minister for Economic Affairs and Finance (Case 48/74)	Member states required to organise a common policy on a disputed tariff area.
1984	Von Colson and Kamann v Land Nordhein-Westfalen (Case 14/83)	National law has to fit Community Law even if it was passed first.

1985	EP v Council (Case 13/83)	Where there is no legal obligation to implement a common policy, associated freedoms must be enforced.
1986	Commission v Italy (Case 101/84)	*Force majeure* (in this case a bomb destroying the records) is no defence to an action under Art.226.
1986	Marshall v South West Area Health Authority (No.I)	National legislation must be interpreted in the light of the wording and purpose of a relevant directive even if not directly relevant.
1986	Netherlands v Reed (Case 59/85)	Freedom of worker movement includes the right of residence to the spouse.
1987	Commission v Council (Case 45/86)	The Council should only use 'catch all' clauses and circumvent the Commission if the treaties don't otherwise provide a more direct treaty basis.
1987	Foto-Frost v Hauptzollamt Lubeck-Ost (Case 314/85)	Only the ECJ, not national courts, may rule that EC law is invalid.
1989	Commission v Germany (Case 249/86)	Freedom of movement extends to workers' families if the worker has certain standards of accommodation.
1989	Commission v UK (Case 221/89R)	The ECJ may assign interim measures.
1990	R. v Secretary of State for Transport Ex p. Factortame (Case C-213/89)	A national law is inferior to EC law and policy.
1990	Marleasing SA v La Commercial Internacional de Alimtacion SA (Case C-106/89)	National provisions must not make it excessively difficult to exercise EC rights.
1990	Barber v. Guardian Royal Exchange (Case 262/88)	ECJ overruled a Council response to an earlier ECJ ruling (Bilka Kaufhaus GmbH v. von Hartz, Case 170/84) while subsequently allowing a financial get-out in limiting back-payments/damages.

Year	Case	Ruling
1991	*Francovich, Bonifaci and others v Italy* (Cases C-6 & 9/90)	States can be financially liable for breaches of EC law, even where there is no direct effect.
1991	Commission v Council (Case C-300/89)	Where the Treaty confers a specific task on the Commission, it also confers on it the necessary powers to achieve it.
1994	Germany V Parliament and Council (C-233/94)	Simple reference to current policy failure in itself demonstrated that the subsidiarity principle had been applied.
1995	*Union des Associations Europeenes de Football v Jean-Marc Bosnian* (Case C-415/93)	An extension of EC equality laws.
1996	R. v Minister of Agriculture, Fisheries and Food Ex p. Hedley Lomas (Ireland) Ltd (Case C-5/94)	A member state may not act unilaterally to avoid a breach of EC law by another member state.
1996	P v S (Case C-13/94)	(On transsexuals) Persons in similar situations should be treated alike unless differential treatment can be objectively justified.
1996	UK v Council (The Working Time Directive) (Case C-84/94)	Endorsed the subversion of subsidiarity by allowing working time regulations to be passed through QMV on health and safety grounds.[4]
2001	Metallgesellschaft Ltd, Hoechst Ag and Hoechst UK v Commissioners of Inland Revenue and H.M. Attorney General (Joined Cases C-379/98 & C-410/98)	A member state can be liable for non-implementation of a directive.
2005	Commission v Council (C-176/03)	Exclusive Commission competence to draft EU environmental criminal laws.
2007	Microsoft Corp. v Commission of the European Communities (T-201/04)	The Commission's decision to impose massive fines on foreign companies on competition grounds – based on basic product construct rather than geographical location – is confirmed.

2009	Ireland v Parliament and Council (C-301/06)	Data retention can be done under QMV single market rules even when undertaken on non-QMV JHA reasons.
2011	Association belge des Consommateurs Test-Achats ASBL and Others v Conseil des ministres (C-236/09)	Gender equality extended.
2014	United Kingdom v Parliament and Council (C-270/12)	Confirmed EU quango's powers to override national financial supervisors to regulate or prohibit short-selling, contrary to lack of legal base.
2014	United Kingdom v Council (C 209/13)	Initial ruling on legality of Financial Transaction Tax: Enhanced Cooperation rules trump non-Eurozone countries' right to be unaffected.

APPENDIX B –
A Submission to the Balance of Competences Review (EU Budget Chapter) by Council of Europe Members

The Other Strasbourg

Britain's Balance of Competences Review: A View from the Council of Europe

The United Kingdom government is currently engaged in an audit of the competences of the European Union, reviewing the impact of the EU treaties. We are parliamentary delegates to the Council of Europe, with a vantage point reaching out across our shared continent. As such we have experience in models of international democratic cooperation.

It is not the first time members of the Assembly have offered their views to the debates and reviews on European integration involving the Treaty of Rome and its successors. During the Convention on the Future of Europe, several of our colleagues submitted a paper reflecting on the view from Strasbourg.[5] We follow in that tradition today.

A Tale of Two Europes

The Council of Europe predates the EU, predates the EC, and predates the EEC. It was founded in 1949 as a mechanism for intergovernmental cooperation across the continent. Delegates are selected from national parliaments, enjoying a more direct link with the electorate. There is no large civil service. There is no powerful community of Commissioners. Decisions are made collectively, rather than through qualified and complex weighted voting. The Council's budget is comparatively modest, rather than equivalent to that of a country in its own right.

As such, it operates on an entirely different model from that of the European Union. We would suggest that in terms of simple cost efficiency and democratic accountability, the intergovernmental approach is better. A study of the attitudes of Britain's founding fathers of European Cooperation, especially Churchill and Bevin who both appreciated the long term direction of events, certainly underlines that view.

A History of Subversion

The European Union has long been assuming the mantle of the Council of Europe through assimilating its identity. It has seen this as a fight for sole legitimacy. The concept of a European anthem was first adopted by the Council, which picked Beethoven's Ode to Joy before it was subsequently adopted by the institutions of the Community. The current EU flag was created for the Council of Europe, and again hijacked by Brussels. An end symptom is that our institution has since had to design a new stand-alone European flag to distinguish our work from the cuckoo's.

This might be a minor annoyance except that the principle is symbolic. For an organisation that is so involved in fighting over intellectual property rights and copyright theft, the EU's approach is rather paradoxical. Yet the mentality is repeatedly one of the EU being the 'true' European cause which rides roughshod over the interests of members of the Council. Time and time again colleagues find MEPs who consider themselves as the sole democratic representatives of the continent of Europe on the international stage, mandated to draw more powers to themselves from member states and to represent the broader continent internationally. This, it has to be said, is largely because of the significant budgets that they already have such control over.

But we would encourage those studying the division of EU competences to delve into the historical archives held across government departments, and the discussions that were taking place over the decades on the relative roles of the two institutions. Indeed, we would recommend compiling these archives and putting them into the public domain.

The result will be to better appreciate the long-term ambitions of those establishing the two types of institutions, where they led, the temporary nature of their setbacks and blocks, and how from today they will continue to expand in years to come. In the story of European cooperation versus integration, context is everything, and timelines explain the dangers of the future.

In that context, the Council of Europe provides a useful safeguard as the international forum of choice. We would encourage you to reflect upon the parallel of the role of the constitutional monarch in your democracy, or of the constitutional president in other systems. Such an individual fills a position without the ability to usurp power. Restoring the Council of Europe closer to a central role in continental cooperation similarly reduces the enduring threat of powers being taken away by a growing federal entity.

The Democratic Deficit

The Laeken Mandate was agreed by the EU's heads of government, as a response to a series of referenda in which those supporting further integration had been badly mauled. As a result of these votes, even the most ardent federalist had to admit that there was a clear disconnect between voters and their elected representatives.

That gap has continued and indeed got wider, as the reactions to the EU Constitution and the Lisbon Treaty showed. Meanwhile, a failure by a number of governments to address citizens' concerns over such issues as immigration, exacerbated in some cases by movement rights under the EU treaties, has contributed to an atmosphere in which extremist groups can more readily find support.

The Council of Europe was set up to avoid such tyrannies and extremisms from arising again. Our work in consequence is being undermined by the activities of the European Union.

Those speaking for European integration as a political project, aiming for full geostrategic integration, are often those least capable of claiming a mandate. European Commissioners are nominees to what amounts to a quango, typically appointed after completing a career in politics (meaning paradoxically that to qualify they have to have lost an election). MEPs are appointed on the basis of a party nomination, through a list system and a form of proportional vote, across a region or nation: this is problematic in that it does not generate a sense of ownership of the politician amongst 'his' voters.

Meanwhile, the EU's Council of Ministers operates under a system that the Commission now estimates is 80 per cent Qualified Majority Voting. Ministers may have to report back to their parliament to say that they wanted something but were forced to do something else by other countries, and there is nothing they can do about it. This palpable failure is consequently masked by a voting abstention.

Quite why anyone should be surprised that ordinary voters should feel outraged at their own impotence is a mystery. Once again, it encourages them to turn to anyone who can provide an answer, however extreme, because the EU system itself makes dishonest people out of those entering its politics.

By contrast, representatives from the Council of Europe are representatives of national parliaments and bear a far greater appreciation of grassroots concerns, public opinions and mood, and carry direct responsibility to a closer electorate.

Ever Closer Union

The EEC/EC/EU approach is based on the principle of countries gradually merging. Participating member states sign up to a political direction that simply does not exist in the Council of Europe model.

This means that for countries that do not wish to become part of a federal superstate down the line, or surrender more powers to central control and QMV, the EU model is a poor choice.

The Council of Europe demonstrates that this approach is not the only one on offer. Other economic groupings, particularly the EEA, EFTA and other bilateral deals between the EU and non-member states, show the economic alternatives also already available that do not carry so great a political burden. In particular, we would encourage revisiting the example of CEFTA and the Visegrad experience as a case study.

The EU treaties specifically cater for the existence of states and groups of states existing beyond its increasingly communal borders. Thanks to the 'Good Neighbour Clause' in the Lisbon Treaty, the EU for the first time recognises that over the long term it has a finite reach for expansion and that there is room for cooperating on a different, non-integrationist level with countries it has not absorbed.

This new development should be grasped with both hands.

Budgetary Blues

The budget of the EU is larger than the GDP of 11 of its member states; and larger than the government budgets of all but nine EU members, that is to say two thirds of them.

By contrast, the Council of Europe achieves what it does on a budget a tiny fraction of that. In practical terms, the entire spending of the CoE is the equivalent of *one half of one day's spending* by the European Union. The *total* figure runs to just the MEPs' admin costs for Strasbourg, including their (symptomatic) Brussels commute.

But management of this huge sum by the EU has been notoriously bad. For approaching two decades the EU's own Court of Auditors has consistently refused to sign off the vast majority of the accounts. OLAF, the in-house criminal investigation agency, is openly running a triage system because it can only handle a portion of the cases it gets pointed to. Parts of the budget have levels of misspending on a par with state social security spending, notorious as the worst part of national budget loss.

A key problem is one of propriety and property. To those dealing with 'EU money' it has not come from any taxpayer, but been magicked out of thin air. There is no sense of ownership, nor guilt at any waste or loss.

We would encourage those undertaking the review to consider the relative efficiencies that go with taking an intergovernmental approach, especially for a net EU budget contributor such as the UK. Duplication should be abandoned, and where it exists the preference should be away from a federal institution. Some fairly challenge the value for money generated by having a Congress of Regional and Local Authorities, costing the CoE €6 million a year. Yet even that sum is less than just the tax revenue from salaries and pension contributions for staff at its EU counterpart that fulfils the same job. So the wider question is why €89 million should be spent on maintaining a Committee of the Regions for the EU as well, which is itself duplicating the work done by MEPs. This is not the only down side. To quote one recent rapporteur, 'reinventing existing norms and setting up parallel [EU] structures creates double standards and opportunities for "forum shopping", which leads to new dividing lines in Europe.'[6]

A Bigger, Truer Europe

'Europe' does not end on the EU's borders. There is no 'Swiss Sea' in the middle of the continent. The Urals have not been excised from de Gaulle's famous dictum at the other extreme from the Atlantic. Nor for that matter do we now bin the continent's spiritual and physical offshoots in the New World and Southern oceans, whose young men travelled to their forefathers' homes to support the democracies in their times of trouble.

'Europe' is bigger than the EU – geographically, spiritually, economically, psychologically. The truth is easy to forget, but only half of the Council's members are EU countries. Only roughly half again of those have merged their currencies. The euro, and economic assimilation, is a minority activity.

Over the coming years, many EU opinion leaders will be put on the spot as the prospect of treaty changes loom through the fog. The 'EU within the EU', the Eurozone, will cause many to reflect on what it means to be part of the political experiment of federal integration. The United Kingdom's activities merely place it at the vanguard of these debates, having identified the problems and issues first.

We simply recommend to those undertaking such critically important studies to look at the history of the project to date and reflect whether the direction is truly the one they want to travel in, or whether an intergovernmental approach is better. They should consider that the alternative to being part of a federal Europe is not to be alone. It is to have a different and equally valid working relationship with our broader European family.

Brian Binley, MP
Davit Harutyunyan, MP
David TC Davies, MP

APPENDIX C – Some Major Examples of UK Gold Plating EU Legislation (in just one field)

Employment Directive	Summary of Directive	Gold-plating
Working Time Directive	Regulates working hours, nightwork, rest breaks and annual leave.	Directive only specifies 'up-to-date records' of all workers who have signed the opt-out. UK regulations require records which show hours worked and for those records to be kept for two years.

Employment Directive	Summary of Directive	Gold-plating
Working Time Directive	Regulates working hours, nightwork, rest breaks and annual leave.	UK regulations allow workers to withdraw from opt-out with only seven days' notice. This is not required by the Directive.
Pregnant Workers Directive	Protects women who are pregnant, have recently given birth or are breast-feeding by giving them at least 14 weeks' maternity leave plus other entitlements.	UK regulations allow women to resign the day they are due to return from maternity leave, making it difficult for employers to plan ahead – the Directive says nothing on this.
Part-Time Work Directive	Prohibits less favourable treatment of part-time workers compared to full-time workers.	UK has not used an exemption in the Directive for casual work.
Part-Time Work Directive	Prohibits less favourable treatment of part-time workers compared to full-time workers.	UK regulations give part-time workers the right to request a written statement of reasons if they believe that they have been less favourably treated than a full-time worker, with the employer obliged to respond within 21 days. This is not required by the Directive.
Fixed Term Work Directive	Prohibits less favourable treatment of fixed-time workers compared to full-time workers.	UK regulations give fixed-time workers the right to request a written statement of reasons if they believe that they have been less favourably treated than a full-time worker, with the employer obliged to respond within 21 days. This is not required by the Directive.
Information on Individual Employment Conditions Directive	Employers must notify new employees of essential aspects of employment contract within two months of starting.	UK has not used an exemption in the Directive for employees who work less than eight hours a week.

Employment Directive	Summary of Directive	Gold-plating
Collective Redundancies Directive	Employers making 20+ redundancies must inform and consult employee representatives, and notify government authorities.	Directive only says consultation must start 'in good time'; UK law stipulates at least 30 days before dismissals take effect, but 90 days where there are 100+ redundancies. The 90 day period could be shortened to 30 days.
Posting of Workers Directive	Minimum terms and conditions laid down by law must apply to employees temporarily posted from another member state.	UK has not used the exemption in the Directive for postings of less than one month.
Equal Opportunities and Treatment of Men and Women Directive	Prohibits discrimination on grounds of sex. Also gives mothers the right to return to the same or an equivalent job after maternity leave.	UK regulations allow compensation for injury to feelings. This is not required by the Directive.
Equal Opportunities and Treatment of Men and Women Directive	As above.	Directive allows an upper limit on compensation in relation to job applications, but this was not incorporated into UK regulations.
Equal Opportunities and Treatment of Men and Women Directive	As above.	Directive allows employer to offer a mother returning from maternity leave equivalent job, rather than keep actual job open. UK regulations require employer to keep job open for six months, and only allow an equivalent job after six months.
Equal Treatment irrespective of Racial or Ethnic Origin Directive	Prohibits discrimination on grounds of race or ethnic origin.	UK regulations allow compensation for injury to feelings. This is not required by the Directive.
Framework for Equal Treatment in Employment Directive	Prohibits discrimination on grounds of religion or belief, disability, age or sexual orientation with regard to recruitment, etc.	UK regulations allow compensation for injury to feelings. This is not required by the Directive.

Employment Directive	Summary of Directive	Gold-plating
Framework for Equal Treatment in Employment Directive	Requires employers to make reasonable accommodation for disabled employees unless it would impose a 'disproportionate burden' on the employer.	UK regulations go beyond Directive. They require an employer to make 'reasonable adjustments' to prevent substantial disadvantage to disabled employees – there is no reference to disproportionate burdens.

Source: "Does the Government 'Gold-Plate' EU Employment Directives?" Alistair Tebbit, Institute of Directors, 2010. But for a wider appreciation see the more recent IoD publication *The Midas Touch* (2013)

APPENDIX D – The Usurpation of the FCO by Brussels on the International Stage

On an operational level, the Commission and the UN had signed a Financial and Administrative Framework Agreement, allowing for direct liaison in the management of programmes. This means the Commission is the key partner on a day-to-day basis for the operational aspects of running how money is spent in programmes run with the UN Secretariat, including: the Department of Political Affairs, the Department for Disarmament Affairs, the Department of Peacekeeping Operations (the United Nations Mine Action Service), the Department of Economic and Social Affairs, the United Nations Conference on Trade and Development, the Office for the Coordination of Humanitarian Affairs, the Office on Drugs and Crime, the Office of the United Nations Security Coordinator, the Economic Commission for Africa, the Economic Commission for Europe, the Economic Commission for Latin America and the Caribbean, the Economic and Social Commission for Asia and the Pacific, the Economic and Social Commission for Western Asia, the Office of the United Nations High Commissioner for Human Rights, the Office of the High Representative for the Least Developed Countries, Landlocked Developing Countries and Small Islands Developing States.

Then there is **UNICEF; UNDP** – the United Nations Development Programme; **UNIFEM** – the United Nations Development Fund for Women; **UNV** – United Nations Volunteers; **UNRWA** – the United Nations Relief and Works Agency for Palestine Refugees in the Near East; **UNHCR** – the Office of the United Nations

High Commissioner for Refugees; **UNFPA** – the United Nations Population Fund; **UNEP** – the United Nations Environment Programme; **UN-HABITAT** – the United Nations Human Settlements Programme; **UNDCP** – the United Nations Drug Control Programme; **CICP** – the Centre for International Crime Prevention; **ITC** – the International Trade Centre; **UNU** – the United Nations University; **UNITAR** – the United Nations Institute for Training and Research; **UN-INSTRAW** – the United Nations Research and Training Institute for the Advancement of Women; and the World Food Programme.

Thanks to bilateral agreements this list also now includes the Preparatory Commission for the Comprehensive Nuclear-Test-Ban Treaty Organization; the Food and Agriculture Organization of the United Nations; the International Atomic Energy Agency; the International Civil Aviation Organization; the International Fund for Agricultural Development; the International Labour Organisation; the International Telecommunication Union; the United Nations Capital Development Fund; the United Nations Educational, Scientific and Cultural Organization; the United Nations Industrial Development Organization; the United Nations Office for Project Services; United Nations Women; the World Health Organization; and the World Meteorological Organization.

That list is just with respect to the UN's working groups, and leaves aside advances made since Resolution A/65/276, upgrading the status of the European Union's participation in the United Nations – and indeed the relationship as it runs in reverse, since at last count the UN had no fewer than 17 diplomatic missions accredited to the EU in Brussels.

To these we can add a significant body of other international organisations. Top of the list is the WTO. This reaches its decisions by consensus, yet the UK is represented by the EU which first reaches its own stance largely through QMV. The UK's global trading interests are thus *diminished* by EU membership on current terms, not enhanced.

There is also a large number of other organisations run outside of the UN and WTO. For example, the European Commission is associated with the Wassenaar Arrangement, as the EC Regulation 1334/2000 sets up a Community regime for the control of exports of dual-use goods and technologies. The EU has quasi-member status at the OECD, and is a full member of its Development Assistance Committee (DAC). The Commission operates as an observer in the Nuclear Suppliers Group (NSG). It is a member of the OSPAR Commission covering the environment in the north east Atlantic. It represents the whole of the EU in such organisations as the North East Atlantic Fisheries Organisation, with the same voting power as Greenland (represented through a quirk by Denmark acting independently).

If we just look at international organisations headquartered in Switzerland, we find the Commission is an Observer at the European Organization for Nuclear Research (CERN) and the International Organization for Migration, while it has been given the special status of 'regional economic integration organisation' at the Intergovernmental Organization for International Carriage by Rail. But it is also a full member of the International Union for the Protection of New Varieties of Plants, and it is a council member at the Geneva International Centre for Humanitarian Demining. It selects three of Europe's five seats on the World Anti-Doping Agency. As a leading member of Eurocontrol, the EU is indirectly represented on SITA (Airlines Worldwide Telecommunications and Information Services). Plus it is double-hatted on the board and represented by a national delegate in the GAVI Alliance (Global Alliance for Vaccines and Immunization), and the Global Fund to Fight Aids, Tuberculosis and Malaria. Moreover, the President of the ECB tends to serve on the Board of Directors of the Bank for International Settlements, while the European Parliament is an associate member of the Inter-Parliamentary Union.

This list, it must be remembered, is partial and dynamic. More details on this process can be found in the TaxPayers' Alliance paper *EU Diplomats*, and in occasional useful features at *EUReferendum.com*.

APPENDIX E – Key Welfare Benefits by EU Country

Country	Health care?	Child Benefit?	Unemployment Benefit?	Housing Benefit?
Austria	Available immediately, but only if you pay 'social insurance' Available after a year	Immediate payment of £89 per month	Only available to people who have paid social insurance	No
Belgium	Available after a year	£115 a month, available immediately	Have to have previously worked in Belgium	No national scheme; amounts vary regionally
Bulgaria	Free emergency care immediately; other treatments only available if you pay social insurance	Targeted schemes restricted to Bulgarian citizens	Minimum of nine months of working in the country required to qualify	Immediate monthly allowance but only if you have a local authority home already

APPENDICES

Country	Health care?	Child Benefit?	Unemployment Benefit?	Housing Benefit?
Cyprus	Free, available immediately	Immediate yearly payment of £444	Six months of work in Cyprus required to qualify	Immediately available, limited to £506 a month
Czech Republic	Cash charges apply	£23 a month available immediately	12-month minimum qualifying period	Available immediately
Denmark	Free, available immediately	Up to £161 a month available after 12 months	Minimum of one year's work required to qualify	No
Estonia	Cash payments required for some treatments	£16 per month available immediately	£12.50 per week available immediately	No
Finland	Flat-rate fees	£88 per month available immediately	Basic weekly unemployment allowance available after two months	Up to 80 per cent of housing costs available immediately but system varies regionally
France	Only available with a card proving entitlement, issued to residents	Immediate payment, but only for parents with more than one child	Four-month qualifying period	Immediate; scheme based on house size and local factors
Germany	Only available with a health insurance card	£155 per month available immediately	Means tested allowance for jobseekers who have made 'intensive efforts' to find work	Full amount of housing costs available immediately
Greece	100 days of work required to qualify	No	Minimum of six months of work required to qualify	No
Hungary	Not immediately available	£40.60 per month available immediately	Minimum qualifying period of 360 days	No
Ireland	Free after living in Ireland for three consecutive years, but free immediately to UK citizens	£110 per month available immediately	£160 per week available immediately	Immediate rent supplement providing short-term support
Italy	Free, available immediately	No	Qualifying period of three months	No national scheme; varies according to region

Country	Health care?	Child Benefit?	Unemployment Benefit?	Housing Benefit?
Latvia	Fees for GP and hospital visits	Immediate monthly payment of £9.30	One-year qualifying period	Varies locally
Lithuania	Three months qualifying period but 'urgent care' free immediately	Immediate monthly payment of £24	18-month qualifying period	No
Luxembourg	Insurance-based	£157.10 per month available immediately	Minimum of six months of work required to qualify	Immediate rent allowance of up to £104.90
Malta	Free, available immediately	Immediate payment; up to £81.55 a month	Immediate means-tested benefit of up to £16 per day	No
Netherlands	Only available with a certificate proving entitlement	Immediate payment of £943 per year	Six-month qualifying period	Means tested, available immediately
Poland	Free, available immediately	Immediate payment of up to £54 per month	Qualifying period of one year	No
Portugal	Free, available immediately	Monthly payment of up to £40	Qualifying period of 180 days	No
Romania	Six-month qualifying period, except for emergencies	Monthly payment of up to £20	Minimum qualifying period of 12 months	No
Slovakia	Nominal cash payment	Immediate monthly payment of £19	Minimum two-year qualifying period	No
Slovenia	Minimum of 10 per cent of some treatment costs	Immediate payment of up to £97 per month	Minimum contribution of nine months	Only available if you already have social housing
Spain	Only available with a card proving entitlement	Immediate payment of up to £20 per month	Immediate payment available based on a variable proportion of average wages	No
Sweden	Basic fees for care	Immediate monthly payment of £101	Six-month qualifying period	Immediate monthly allowance of up to £125

Country	Health care?	Child Benefit?	Unemployment Benefit?	Housing Benefit?
United Kingdom	Free of charge under NHS	Paid immediately if the child is under 16, or 16 to 19 and in education or training, and the claimant has an individual income of less than £50,000. Amount is £20.30 a week for the eldest or only child, £13.40 per additional child	Immediate payment of £71.70 a week in Jobseeker's Allowance (JSA) after proving you are actively seeking work. EU migrants have to pass the 'right-to-reside' test to show they are 'economically active'. The European Commission wants to abolish this test. There is also contribution-based additional JSA which is only available after working for at least two years	Available immediately if you are on a low income, whether you are working or unemployed. How much depends on individual circumstances, but amount cannot normally exceed £250 per week for a one-bedroom property, or up to £400 a week for four bedrooms or more

Sources: *European Commission guides to social security and health care in member states, Organisation for Economic Co-operation and Development, Department for Work and Pensions.* Data compiled by *Daily Telegraph*, 19 October 2013

The overall UK bill is exacerbated by the triple factors of a comparatively high cost of living (meaning higher social security to compensate); the high number of economic migrants compared with other EU member states; and by the failure of NHS managers to reclaim money owed under EHIC health arrangements.

APPENDIX F – Value of the UK Rebate Over Time

Year	Actual value of UK rebate in nominal prices (ECU/€m)	Actual value of UK rebate in nominal prices (£m)	Amount lost because of 2005 reforms in nominal prices (€m)	Amount lost because of 2005 reforms in nominal prices (£m)	Value of UK rebate had 2005 changes not been made in nominal prices (ECU/€m)	Value of UK rebate had 2005 changes not been made in nominal prices (£m)
1985	386	227	-	-	386	227
1986	2,534	1,701	-	-	2,534	1,701
1987	1,636	1,153	-	-	1,636	1,153
1988	2,399	1,594	-	-	2,399	1,594
1989	1,718	1,154	-	-	1,718	1,154
1990	2,376	1,697	-	-	2,376	1,697
1991	3,563	2,497	-	-	3,563	2,497
1992	2,562	1,881	-	-	2,562	1,881
1993	3,262	2,539	-	-	3,262	2,539
1994	2,230	1,726	-	-	2,230	1,726
1995	1,473	1,207	-	-	1,473	1,207
1996	3,007	2,412	-	-	3,007	2,412
1997	2,515	1,733	-	-	2,515	1,733
1998	2,052	1,378	-	-	2,052	1,378
1999	4,817	3,171	-	-	4,817	3,171
2000	3,421	2,085	-	-	3,421	2,085
2001	7,333	4,560	-	-	7,333	4,560
2002	4,928	3,099	-	-	4,928	3,099
2003	5,097	3,559	-	-	5,097	3,559
2004	5,296	3,593	-	-	5,296	3,593
2005	5,349	3,656	-	-	5,349	3,656
2006	5,236	3,569	-	-	5,236	3,569
2007	5,149	3,523	-	-	5,149	3,523
2008	6,114	4,862	302	240	6,416	5,102
2009	6,057	5,392	1,350	1,202	7,407	6,594
2010	3,553	3,047	2,117	1,816	5,670	4,863
2011	3,623	3,143	2,355	2,043	5,978	5,186
2012	3,835	3,110	2,891	2,344	6,726	5,454
2013	4,073 (est.)	3,324 (est.)	3,407	2,780	7,480 (est.)	6,104 (est.)
Total	105,594	76,591	12,422	10,425	118,016	87,016

Source: Business for Britain Briefing Note [7]
Note: these figures are originally calculated in euros, and exclude inflation.

APPENDIX G – A Proposed Formula to Calculate Benefits from Full EU Membership

$$5a = \frac{f1+f2+f3}{f4+f5+f6} + \frac{s1}{s2} + \frac{\omega}{d+f7} + \frac{p1}{p2+t} + f8$$

a is the end sum in question, consisting of five parts to be taken into consideration – hence 5a. The top side of the fraction (the numerator) supplies advantages of membership, the bottom side (or denominator) the negatives; so added together a figure larger than a baseline of 1 indicates membership is advantageous to a particular state.

f1 represents the increased trade stimulated by membership of the trading bloc; *f2* the production advantages gained due to standardisation; *f3* the administrative benefits accruing from decreased red tape. However, against these have to be set *f4*, the net 'membership' cost of the UK-EU budget deficit; *f5* or the combined red tape costs as well as the incidental costs of running individual policies, such as the damage inflicted upon coastal communities as well as the consumer by the CFP; and *f6*, the benefits that would accrue in trade terms anyway from the WTO, GATT, and other instruments that would make the EU gains redundant.

The second element relates to the more abstract concept of sovereignty. This sets *s1* or the beneficial impact of 'pooled sovereignty in a globalised world' against *s2*, the negative impact of the sovereignty lost. This is an area for assessment rather than mathematics.

The third element is one of the big picture, ω, represents the aspirational end status of the EU, and the end process of salami slicing. While this does carry with it substantial positives, there are also major negatives, represented as *d* and *f7*. The former is the very real loss of democratic accountability that arises inherently from the process. The accompanying financial element, *f7*, provides our shorthand for the fraud and waste that is encouraged by this distance.

Next, there is the element relating to 'Peace in Europe'. *p1* represents the concept that the European 'process' has brought political and military stability to the continent, and adds value to a nation's security today. Against this, we set *p2* which postulates that peace has been achieved notwithstanding the

EEC/EC/EU, but rather through NATO, a divided Germany, and the Soviet threat. t meanwhile represents the action of time cementing the habits of peace.

Finally, there is the alternative element. Set against an underlying standard baseline of 1, $f8$ represents the departure costs for a state of leaving the EU, which will vary depending on the manner and good will surrounding withdrawal.

This then provides us with our five fractions: the financial; sovereignty; the strategic destination; peace and stability; and the alternative route. Combined, they provide one way of assessing whether any given state is better off in or out. Someone should be officially calculating them.

Lee Rotherham

Endnotes

Chapter 1

1. Speech of the Prime Minister, Bloomberg, 23 January 2013

2. See the commentary on this in *Plan B for Europe: Lost Opportunities in the EU Constitution Debate* (online at the Bruges Group website). These negotiations provide salutary lessons on how we might expect renegotiation talks to pan out. On the repatriation of powers issue, the Commission was initially prepared to accept some powers going back, until it recognised that the majority of delegates wanted certain individual powers to go in the other direction. Collectively that meant more integration and the Commission happily ran with this.

3. It is worth recalling the observation contained in the internal FCO audit of the 1973-5 renegotiation and referendum: 'In early 1974, faced with the election of a Government committed to the policy set out in the Manifesto, the other governments reacted with hostility and distrust. They attached importance to British membership, but they were not prepared to compromise on the principles of the Community in order to maintain it. It was almost impossible to guess how much they would be prepared to give away' (Declassified Spreckley Report, pp 4-5). Much of this report deserves close study. The role of the civil service in keeping ministers from actions that risked triggering 'accidental' exit during the negotiations is particularly notable; as is the official tactic of pitching for easily-attainable red lines; the co-option of third parties; and the manner in which Eurosceptic ministers were outmanoeuvred within the Whitehall system.

4. The end results in either eventuality might very usefully remain subject to a confirmatory referendum. Given the political momentum of integration, a No vote should, we suggest, signify support for Article 50 exit rather than acceptance of sovereign entropy.

5. Some might challenge this on the grounds of practicality, referencing for instance the example of the role of Rhode Island in vetoing tariff reform in early post-independence United States history. But the UK is not Rhode Island, the EU is not the United States, and for democracy to function requires representatives at some level to have the freedom to endorse or to block laws a majority of their constituents disagree with.

6. Going up after the Lisbon changes finally take effect, but so too is the QMV threshold.

7. See *Britain and the ECHR*, published by the Tax Payers' Alliance, which explores the options on offer. The anniversary of the signing of Magna Carta provides a ready date shortly after the General Election to announce that human rights are being fixed, to become more about *rights and responsibilities* and on a more basic level.

8. *Lawyers, Judges and the Making of a Transnational Constitution*, American Journal of International Law, January 1981. An early observation in the piece that is often overlooked is that (unlike the ECHR) no dissenting opinion or minority view is allowed, which is of itself indicative of the nature of the construct. Other trade tribunals also allow for this, but their remits are more claustrophobic.

9. *The Transformation of Europe*, Joseph Weiler, The Yale Law Journal, June 1991

10. Work by Swiss MP Andreas Gross at the Council of Europe (where he is the Socialist Group leader) provides a fascinating counterpoint, since he comes from a pro-European perspective and uses the Swiss federal model as a defining and limiting power. The definition of a 'federal Europe' as a threat to UK sovereignty has been a bit of a Eurosceptic misnomer: the real threat

is the direction coupled with the lack of limitation, rather than the definition of powers. This is something to be fair the Lib Dems sometimes admit - though their end goals like those of Mr Gross involve a huge transfer of sovereignty that would be fatal to the nation state. Annex B contains a submission to the Balance of Competences review by CoE members that may be more to the reader's liking.

11 The example of the Mediaeval French courts may appear a peculiar one to raise, but it proves a strangely apt if barely understood parallel (as indeed does the Papal Rota of Avignon, and the English response of *Praemunire*). The argument was over the contrasting sovereignty of the English Crown in Gascony – French territory – as operating under the separate higher jurisdiction of the French Crown. The issue of appeals to Paris rather than the Ducal court at Bordeaux was essentially the trigger for the entire Hundred Years' War, and remained the unresolved issue that fanned enduring discontent even during periods of supposed peace. Indeed, Paris deliberately fostered discontent by encouraging vexatious vassals to appeal to it, thus undoing the tremendous territorial gains made under Edward III. The legal conflict was only resolved with the loss by the English Crown of the territories concerned 116 years later, that is to say by the political destruction of one of the two competing judiciaries.

Chapter 2

1 The IEA has done outstanding work on this subject. See in particular *Euro Puppets: The European Commission's Remaking of Civil Society*, Christopher Snowden, February 2013. HMG is also variously guilty of this technique: it remains an abuse of taxpayer money as well as a needless bounty for socialist lobbyists. If there were one enduring legacy the Coalition could leave to good governance from what remains of its term of office, it should be to end this charade.

2 See in particular Alter's paper *The European Court's Political Power Across Time and Space*, Northwestern University School of Law Faculty Paper, 2009, which sets out some ground markings in relation to these 'interested litigants'.

3 Exactly the same problem affects ECHR judge appointments. At least in this instance MPs vet them. In practice though, the three candidates display similar backgrounds and credentials, and even if they have such views, prudently they never flag up that they have a track record of opposing anything that might disqualify them as being too much a stalwart of national sovereignty. We are not terribly optimistic either of the number of MPs at the Council of Europe who do actually read their CVs.

4 Some attempt to refute the claim that Brussels is essentially a supranational entity by claiming it has fewer civil servants working for it than, say, Birmingham. Apart from overlooking the number of Brummy street cleaners not on the Commission's pay roll, this forgets a basic truth: like the Raj before it, Brussels operates as a bolt-on hierarchy, issuing top-down instructions for others to implement. It does not need to be massive, though its importance is reflected in its wages (a difference that however does mark it out from, say the handful of élite administrators of the imperial Sudan).

5 European Scrutiny Committee, Westminster, 24th Report, Nov 2013, available online.

6 We return to the EEA later. The Scrutiny Committee's suggested pre-requirement that parliament can only veto an EU law if its own government had formally voted against it is not, as it happens, matched as an obligation for EEA parliaments.

7 In fact, Conservative policy in opposition under several spokesmen was actually to abrogate the Common Fisheries Policy.

8 For example, 2007/60/EC. This pushed the Environment Agency into managing floods rather than preventing them, years before Owen Paterson's appointment.

NOTES

Chapter 3

1 Though he has the option. John Redwood did as a minister. We would recommend all ministers who go to Council of Ministers meetings use this right at least once during their tenure.

2 Incidentally, where such proposals do get spiked, they are often classed as 'Euromyths', along with other ideas being discussed in committee which are killed off when they become public and are quickly then seen as toxic. The best definition of a Euromyth is consequently that it is a bad law that Eurosceptics uncover before it gets too far down the legislative pipe to repudiate.

3 Now Articles 114, 115 and 352.

4 The lack of any provision in the treaties has not stopped institutions from pressing on, either through claiming tentative association with a clause of indirect relevance and waiting for the ECJ to rule on it (or the Council of Ministers to simply not object); or by just going ahead without any legal cover at all. This latter was particularly notable with legal basis for Community grants in the 1990s but remains an issue today.

5 European Scrutiny Commitee, Westminster, 29th Report of 2006-7.

6 There may well be individual cases where an additional legal base may be required (for instance, on levying sanctions against the Taleban since they do not constitute a state). But does this actually need to be via the EU or can an agreement be made multilaterally on the fringes of the Council meeting? The Taleban example shows how precedent is set and subsequently expands. Their use is particularly shocking when one considers the supposed parallelism with the US Constitution so bombastically made during the drafting of the European Constitution: the US version does not have such a dangerous mechanism.

7 Up until 2002 disputes were settled bilaterally within a short time frame, otherwise then escalated to the wider council. It now has a *Tribunal Permanente de Revisión*, significantly destined 'para garantizar la correcta interpretación, aplicación y cumplimiento de los instrumentos fundamentales del proceso de Integración' (TPR website). [Trans; to guarantee the correct interpretation, application and compliance with fundamental instruments of the process of integration]

8 Article 20 allows for summits to decide how they want to reach an agreement where an agreement cannot be reached.

9 The Heritage Foundation significantly concludes that post-EU, the UK and US should enter into bilaterals rather than try to arrange extended NAFTA membership.

10 It also of course raises the question whether moving to the EEA arrangement would not be a simpler step while sorting out what deal best suits the UK. If there are issues here, there are other alternatives: see the Freedom Association paper *Manning the Pumps: A Handbook for Salvaging the Eurosceptic Credentials of the Conservative Party* (Rotherham, 2014). A further point though is that the EFTA Court considers the ECHR Court as a source of legal inspiration, which would need to be separately addressed (particularly on residency and employment rights matters).

10 UK access to the EFTA Court as an arbiter in an EEA or EEA+1 environment would fall out from UK application to EFTA prior to departure from the customs union, but might be settled in advance of a third party FTA transition.

12 Particular credit is due to Dr Richard North and Christopher Booker for developing this point. It is also to be hoped that the wider research associated with the Brussels audit led by David Campbell Bannerman MEP will be published, as this expands significantly on the material covered in these paragraphs.

13 *Scoping Study for the Evaluation of EU REACH and CLP Regulations*, RPA study for DEFRA, 2009.

14 European External Action Service Review, 2013, see www.eeas.europa.eu

Chapter 4

1. The concept of a 'Passport Union' (a concept so innovative the Commission recognised it was a neologism) is not an aspect of the original founding treaties nor even of the Treaty of Accession, but emerged from late 1974 onwards as part of early measures to support the concept of a 'European citizenship'. As such it is not part of the original terms but is now, of course, part of the *acquis*.

2. 'David Cameron's EU Speech', BBC website, 28.11.2014

3. Several are on the MigrationWatch website. These should be caveated with recent work by City A.M. but the two vantage points are not in fact mutually exclusive.

4. *Migration Statistics Quarterly Report*, ONS, May 2014

5. The ONS does not seem to have updated the graph since 2012, but the data holds.

6. See http://www.migrationwatchuk.org/pressArticle/83 for a summary.

7. Including indeed reactions to David Blunkett in 2002 ('I didn't say that Britain was being swamped. I was talking about a school or GP practice'), and Margaret Thatcher in 1978 ('People are really rather afraid that this country might be rather swamped by people with a different culture'). To these we can now add the recent (26 October 2014) comments by Michael Fallon.

8. The statistics are not always helpful in exploring identity, often preferring to focus on original ancestry. This masks the figures for actual 'British' nationality marked not ethnically but by a sense of association and deep attachment. 38% of those so often categorised as 'Indians' in London were in fact born in the UK and actually British.

9. *Eurofacts*, 19 April 2013. This is without reviewing any of the further controversies about also thus encouraging marriages with close degrees of consanguinity across several generations.

10. Though it is a subject of extraordinary significance for this country and for others. An awareness of the history of it would suit legislators well. Roosevelt notably contrasted the US approach during a visit of Mackenzie King (PM of Canada) by pointing out that the French Canadians who had settled in the US had been largely absorbed, despite being as numerous as the ones that had stayed in Canada. FDR was being somewhat blithe given the relative total national population shares, but US immigration policy entailed assimilation within three generations. Long term, the failure to assimilate Hispanoamerican immigration (though slowed down by shifting economic investment patterns following NAFTA) will probably entail the greatest geopolitical shift in North America over the coming century: a Hispanic *revanche des berceaux* is in play that ultimately threatens either to overturn the Treaty of Guadalupe Hidalgo (and subsequently possibly even the Treaty of Paris), or to revisit Bismarck's observation about the key feature of the coming century is about the language spoken by the Americans. In short: abuse immigration for political gain at your national peril.

11. The reader is invited to compare the history of immigration and assimilation in the United States and Australia, further contrasted with the Trudeau experiment of multiculturalism (itself deployed as a political counter to the Anglo-French biculturalism associated with the Canadian model pre-1960s). Labour's policy seems to have transplanted a certain Trudeaunian arrogance and multiplied it to absurd levels, taking tactics abused on a half continent and applying them to a densely populated island.

12. A British identity might indeed run in parallel to other identities, whether Scottish, Ulster, Welsh, Cornish, Yorkshire, Essex, Jamaican, Australian, or Grenadine for example; but the Tebbit Cricket Test is a reasonable baseline principle to reflect on.

13. See *Britain and the ECHR*, TaxPayers' Alliance. London, 2010. The specific case in question relates to a cocaine smuggler who couldn't be deported as he had HIV and would receive better treatment on the NHS.

NOTES

14   We may predict a tendency from Whitehall to cite the NOV 14 ECJ ruling of *Elisabeta Dano, Florin Dano v Jobcenter Leipzig* (C-333/13) to suggest the UK is 'winning the argument'. The judges in that case, however were unequivocal in identifying that the plaintiff had made no attempt to get a job. We can expect few clear cut parallels in further cases (especially now).

15   Most UK expats tend to head towards North America and Australasia. The main exception within the EU is Spain. Crucially, we might therefore expect no major *quid pro quo* threats arising from robust measures taken within the UK on social security issues. In the Spanish case, many recipients arrive already retired and therefore not in employment or seeking it; S1 (as the health card was known) and private health insurance rules largely govern their healthcare (though provincial pay-in schemes now do also operate, and S1 has been discontinued); those that are employed are so in the tourist/holiday industry because of their native English language skills and ready affiliation with the tourist, and therefore cannot be simply replaced by locally-engaged workers; others are in SMEs catering for UK expats and are therefore paying their way in taxes. So even Madrid may be prepared to accept UK changes.

16   A similar wide-ranging table could and should be established for a number of other policy hot potatoes being considered by policy thinkers, starting with crafting a coherent Government response to narcotics.

17   ACPO FOI 000096/12. Tellingly there was no data on how many DAF (Daily Activity File) updates to the Police National Computer (PNC) ended with an actual conviction. We are left working with DAF as the nationality field on court records is at present only filled in if deemed relevant to the case, and such data as exists is not collated centrally. We do know for reference that the nationalities with over 5% notification were Poland (27%), Romania (17%), Italy (15%), Hungary (8%), Latvia (7%) and Portugal (6%). These figures predate EU2 wider labour access, and must be approached with some caution. Any audit comparing levels of criminality as a proportion of migrant workers present could prove more insightful on societal and class grounds since it would have to include analysis of types of workforce, skill sets, expectations of initial employment, labour mobility, options for retrogression to country of origin, and so on. Are Germans at an incredible 0.002% DAF rate because they are largely middle class or work in the City; or is it truly a societal/character mark? The answer would require a volume, but at least from that list we can identify the main countries of origin (much of which will already be evident from the proportion of the EU migrant workforce resident) and which are disproportionately more or less likely to see nationals who offend. An absence of specified charges data is a loss, and reduces us to near-anecdotal review of local newspaper coverage of court summaries. This suggests a predominance of anti-social behaviour issues (cultural gaps, wilful or accidental), and others relating to cost savings (non-payment of vehicle insurance, breach of health and safety, excessive 'hot bunking' in housing and such like).

18   This is the problem of 'Vested Rights'. The example of Greenland and some of the ECJ case law is latterly usefully cited by Gerard Batten MEP and Pavel Stroilov (*The Road to Freedom*, Bretwalda, 2014). We would contend this would only in reality likely apply, unless specifically extended, to EEA nationals *already* resident in the UK. But this still leaves a measure of ambiguity subject to judicial test, and means a residual impact from current failed policies and public expectations would therefore need to be managed – or the legacy rights issue directly addressed as part of the renegotiation process.

Chapter 5

1   The authors would here like to pay particular thanks to Dr Ruth Lea for her invaluable assistance in developing the economic elements of this paper.

2   *TheCityUK*, 'Links between financial markets in the UK and EU', October 2013; and 'UK & the EU: a mutually beneficial relationship', December 2013. On the following points see also; *Fresh*

Start, 'Manifesto for change, a new vision for the UK in Europe', January 2013, which reported that '…our financial services contribute substantially to the EU; they represent 61% of the EU's net exports in financial services and 36% of the financial wholesale market.'

3   With *droit de suite*, this meant pushing UK trade to Switzerland and New York (as opposed to California incidentally, which also has such a law which has signally failed).

4   ESMA is the European Securities and Markets Authority, a Euro-quango based in Paris. The proposal would have removed the ability to set benchmark rates.

5   *Options for Change*, EU Fresh Start, March 2012.

6   Referenced in the Fresh Start paper, *op cit*.

7   For background, see: *The Eurozone is Integrating Politically as the Economies Continue to Deteriorate*, Dr Ruth Lea, Arbuthnot Banking Group, 17 December 2012.

8   *'Genuine Economic and Monetary Union' and the implications for the UK*, House of Lords, European Union Committee, 14 February 2014, press release.

9   John Gapper, 'Europe finally takes its bite from the City of London', *FT*, 21 February 2013.

10 A useful and current study of trends and direction is set out in Business for Britain's June 2014 report, 'EU Financial Regulation'. This is particularly so with regard to the consideration of the EU as shifting from a force of liberalisation towards that of a regulator, including whether this also reduces City opportunities across the single market. It concludes that UK interests over the long term could only be met if there were a fundamental rebalancing of Eurozone and non-Eurozone interests including amendments to existing regulations; this would require a 'very considerable' structural and philosophical change by EU institutions.

11 This is before we get into the issue of the Treasury costs directly associated with matched funding, the deduction that also then follows to the rebate, and the bidding costs for grant applicants themselves (a burden even if successful). Critical but often overlooked are the hidden costs under the rebate maths: in addition to what the Exchequer pays as its half of direct matched grants, the Communities' half of the grant money has often been offset against rebate receipts. Treasury reluctance to support grant bids makes more sense when you thus factor in that it might ultimately be paying not for half of the state aid, but over four fifths. The end result is a situation whereby for instance France will claim €443m for EU-supplied food banks over 2014-20 (under European Aid to the Most Deprived: a long-controversial line), while the UK accepts €4.3m. The total funds available will be €2.5bn. Money accepted by the UK under this scheme would though be removed from structural funds totals which the Treasury deems to have greater cost-benefit.

12 It is unclear but it seems from the documentation that the FCO for 3-4 years after accession may have thought the UK ran a small net surplus, though was aware of and concerned at an obvious fall into major deficit coming at the close of the decade. If so, the disconnect across Whitehall from the financial realities is all the more telling.

13 Cf unambiguous French attitudes on the Strasbourg EP seat, also requiring unanimity to change.

14 General Affairs Council Presidency Press Release, 18 June 2005

15 In an important interview on the eve of the Luxembourg referendum on the EU Constitution, Juncker comes across as a pragmatist from a small country with historically dangerous neighbours he wants to trade with, and seeking to protect his state through the rule of law using integration as that tool. But more significantly for the future, he reveals he opposes the UK (/Dutch) social model and strongly believes in pushing for political integration; he does want the UK to stay a member, by 'helping the British to solve a problem they themselves have created'. Interview, 6 July 2005, http://www.verfassung-fir-europa.lu/fr/actualites/2005/07/06juncker_telecran/index.html

16 HM Treasury, *European Union Finances 2013*

NOTES

17 It may be some consolation to supporters of Gordon Brown that his major dumping of gold (perhaps part-triggered by market mismanagement of gold derivatives by leading banks, though the lesson was not learned) has already now been surpassed in value by Blair's rebate folly. That loss is set to be doubled again over three years.

18 EP written question to the Commission, 15 May 2012, E-004994/2012, Georgios Stavrakakis (S&D) http://www.europarl.europa.eu/sides/getDoc.do?pubRef=-//EP//TEXT+WQ+E-2012-004994+0+DOC+XML+V0//EN

19 Balzani Report, MEPs' Committee on Budgetary Control (2012).

20 Total RAL at end 2011 were running at €3.3bn for UK programmes compared with €13.7bn for Italy, €13.4bn for Spain, and €20.2bn for Poland. RAL liabilities provide for another powerful incentive for the UK to remove itself from the central budget of the EU and operate in a treaty of association, and may act as a potent negotiating tool even stronger than the threat of removing the UK contributions. But the principles and the finances need to be explored in advance by negotiators.

Chapter 6

1 The EU's Social Market model might be seen as the French price for accepting the single market. As such, there is no prospect of reforming it, only escaping it.

2 The exact figure on UK exports to the EU merits a paper in its own right, but assessments variously fall between 9% and 15%. These sums however themselves overlook the Antwerp/Rotterdam Effect (UK exports re-exported globally via these ports), the Amsterdam Effect (use of Dutch holding headquarters masking global ownership) and Ireland Effect (exports to the ROI which has long been a closely associated economy even without the single market); we are inclined towards the lower estimate. The figure also overlooks the incomplete nature of the single market in services presently reducing the value to the UK in export terms of that part of the treaties.

3 The cost of the red tape burden is also highly disputed and is seemingly a missed opportunity by the Balance of Competences Review. But even the Commission itself appears to concede, unintentionally, that comparatively low-EU exporting countries (like the UK) would face more burdens than gain trade advantage. Regulations are costly. Commissioner Gunter Verheugen, whose job was to tackle Brussels red tape, estimated they were equivalent to 5.5% of EU GDP back in 2006 – which is higher than the single market gain.

4 Tellingly, even Switzerland which is landlocked etc. prefers an alternative model to full membership. See the recent TFA paper *Manning the Pumps* by one of the authors which covers this area of relative advantage in greater depth, and to which we later briefly return.

5 The reader is particularly invited to review a major audit on this. *See Britain & Europe: A New Relationship*, Lea and Binley, Global Vision, 2012. This contains deeper analysis of the regulatory issues, and provides the source references for the material in these paragraphs.

6 *Climate Change Act 2008, Impact Assessment*, DECC, March 2009. This IA said that the annual costs could be £14.7-18.3bn annually until 2050, with a total cost (PV) of £324-404bn. The total benefits, somewhat improbably, were expected to exceed the costs.

7 'EU Business Regulation', Business for Britain briefing note. We might also ourselves calculate the figure growing by getting on for 400 words (about a page, say) of *acquis* every hour, which seems about right given the volume of Official Journals that come out. Or used to: they are now only available online.

8 Even were they not, they are banned as Euro civil servants from supporting a national government's position (though this has been infamously honoured in the breach by certain capitals).

9   55 times since 1996, according to stats released by Business for Britain in March 2014. A QMV vote only happens once it is clear that a voting majority is in favour of a measure.

10 'What business thinks', Business for Britain Survey, November 2013

11 The IEC, the International Technical Commission founded in London in 1906 for example, has 174 technical committees and subcommittees working out standards for global norms on electrotechnical issues. However the European Commission instead pushes its proxy, CENELUC, since it (in its own words, and with our emphasis) 'generally supports, in line with its political objectives, the development of a (**preferably regional**) infrastructure for standardisation'. The Commission's preference to prioritise continental free trade over global free trade underlines its priorities for political union, and ought to caution us as we consider our place within EU-based structures.

12 *Cut EU Red Tape: Report from the Business Taskforce*, February 2014

13 Several are in fact merely currently threatened Commission proposals that might not even be formally produced. Any attempt by Whitehall to produce these as negotiating victories would be particularly obvious and shallow.

14 Regulation 492/2009

15 'If all the legislation the EU has passed were laid out lengthways it would be over 120 miles long. Along the M1 it would stretch from London all the way past Nottingham. Even if we just account for the amount of EU legislation currently in force, at 31.7 miles it stretches even further than a marathon and would take the average person more than four hours to run along. The total amount of legislation passed since the start of the EU would be nearly as tall as Nelson's column – 43.8 metres to Nelson's 46m. Even if you were to stack just the 170,000 pages of currently active legislation on top of each other they would reach over 11 metres (36 feet) tall – over twice the height of one of London's old Routemaster double-decker buses, which stood at 4.3 metres (over 29 feet) tall. The weight of the entire Official Journal is over a tonne – equivalent to the size of a small whale or rhinoceros. The total weight of the parts of the Official Journal that are currently in force is 285 kg.' (*Just How Big is the Acquis Communautaire?* OE 2005). This assumes of course that the share of extant legislation is a fair share of the relative sizes of the documents too. But why not?

16 The lion's share of the plum pudding falls to the globally-minded British, though Britain itself rests dangerously on the table, along with Scandinavia by curious further parallel.

17 Christine Lagarde, Dimbleby Lecture, 3 February 2014.

18 See in particular 'The OECD-WTO 'Trade in Value Added' Research: a Breakthrough in Analysing World Trade', Dr Ruth Lea, Artbuthnot Banking Group, 17 February 2014.

19 'The OECD-WTO "Trade in Value Added" Research: a Breakthrough in Analysing World Trade', Dr Ruth Lea, Artbuthnot Banking Group, 17 February 2014.

20 The UK's percentage share had, moreover, dropped by ten points over the previous decade: in itself an indicator of changing trade priorities.

21 *This Blessed Plot: Britain and Europe from Churchill to Blair*, Hugo Young, Overlook Press, 1998.

22 See for example, Sarianna Lundan and Geoffrey Jones, 'The "Commonwealth Effect" and the process of internationalisation', *World Economy* (January 2001). This puts the discussions over Amsterdam and the EU Constitution, going on at the time, into proper perspective.

23 Including over any data that exposes the reliance of other EU members on the UK as a key and resilient non-Eurozone export market, whatever our affiliation status. Acknowledging this also accepts that both sides in any renegotiation have an interest in accepting continued mutual market access to and from the UK, meaning the FCO would itself have to admit the terms of association could be far looser than it has in fact aimed for to date.

24 This is not a recent issue of contention as it happens. The first ever cost-benefit analysis of British accession to a continental political bloc took place during the Principate/very early Empire, a full *two millennia* ago. Strabo (IV, 5) writes that the Britons accepted very heavy tariffs, on luxury trade in particular. In turn this meant that the Roman Treasury would be drained by a policy of annexation, since it would mean the reduction of customs duties from any acquired territories entering the 'customs union', coupled with the need to spend on garrison costs (underestimated even then as it happens). British independence continued for a hundred years as a result of Roman financial self interest, to which we could add the lesser 'goodwill' measures associated with quasi-bilaterals on 'passport controls' (handing over shipwrecked mariners), and JHA issues (not backing insurgents). Actual invasion ultimately followed a century after Caesar's short expeditions and for much the same reasons: political distraction, and economic errors over the prospect of mineral wealth. To these we might speculatively add an awareness of potential dependence on imported foreign grain stocks to supply garrisons on the Rhine; so perhaps we might add a proto-CAP as a cause of the early woes of the 'Brittunculi'.

25 The Balance of Competences Review ran a study looking at the CFP, which appears to be the only reasonably balanced production. However, it excludes (for obvious practical considerations) Owen Paterson's outstanding policy review that he undertook while in Opposition. That itself merits greater appreciation.

26 *The Price of Fish*, TaxPayers' Alliance, 2009

27 High-HP blue water UK vessels were being bought up by foreign (largely Spanish) owners in order to get around EU-set national quotas. The 1997 agreement provided for such vessels to have to meet one of four requirements demonstrating an economic link with the UK. However, the Commission President subsequently wrote to the Spanish Foreign Minister explaining that the arrangement did not significantly change existing rules. Of the set criteria that now needed to be met, the least stringent option was simply that a vessel would have to merely visit a UK port on a majority of occasions before starting to trawl.

28 The example is not unique. The North West Waters have an English Channel working group that is much more orientated towards the fishermen themselves, but the UK has eight members and the French 15.

29 There are more recent documents displaying current ambition, but this one demonstrates a coherent long-term intent.

30 The archaeology aspect should at least provide Commission sponsors with a lesson from history. Continental trade with Britain was so significant it even had its own goddess in Roman times. Nehalennia looked after merchants crossing the North Sea over to Britain from the lower Rhine/Scheldt. Inscriptions to her survive from as far up river as Cologne.

31 The Commission is also brazen about some of its motivation: 'A sense of common identity may well be one important side effect of bringing stakeholders together to participate in maritime planning processes.'

32 As the use of ecological clauses to get the Commission involved in the running of North Sea oil demonstrates.

33 It is simply acknowledging the clear historical precedents demonstrated variously by Iceland, Norway, Greenland and the Faroes and how they are able to manage, prioritise, and safeguard their own waters and stocks.

34 Such as the Nordics grant in the far north. But this should be exceptional and strategic, and not an excuse to break Bastiat's principles.

35 Fallow set aside for nesting song birds and the like.

36 *Food for Thought*, TPA, 2010. The actual bill is obviously variable depending on world food prices (opportunity cost) and level of subsidy in a given year.

37 With the UK no longer covered by the CAP aspects of the treaties, it gains the ability to threaten putting up an anti-EU tariff wall on agricultural products in response to petty single market obstructionism in Brussels. The large disparity across the WTO between permitted industrial and the larger agricultural tariffs may also notably allow for disproportionate and very targeted responses in any trade dispute coming from those members, as it happens, with strong rural lobbies.

38 *A Voice for Millions*, published in the collection *Plan B for Europe* along with a number of other historically important Eurosceptic submissions (available online at the Bruges Group website, but hard copies are also available from the authors of this publication). In addition to William Hague, the signatories included former premiers, senior Cabinet members, Presidential candidates, and party leaders.

39 There is an argument that fish do constitute part of the single market because they swim across different nations' seas, meaning the stocks should be jointly managed. If this was truly a large problem Norway or Iceland should not be able to cope.

40 We believe that actually ending the direction of ever closer union is an impossibility, even if the wording itself is cut. Take for example the Tindemans Report, commissioned by the Council of Ministers to define what was actually meant by 'European Union': 'European Union will be on the right track when the European dimension is constantly in the minds of the decision makers of the Member States, when European action is no longer thought of as an extension of minor and marginal importance of a national policy based on national interests, when European decisions and action are accepted as the normal means of controlling our society and safeguarding the future. Today we must push aside intellectual barriers.' That report dates from 1975, and was seen as a compromise towards the British line! The reality is that integration is genetically and culturally imprinted into the very DNA of Brussels. Halts in ever closer union are reminiscent of the custom spotted by Marco Polo on the Coromandel Coast. The locals observed the Choiach (Tyajya), an astrologically taboo hour variably set according to the day. Checking the time by measuring the length of one's shadow, a merchant might declare 'It is Choiach. Do nothing.' Checking later, 'Choiach is over. Do as you will.' Delays in EU integration deal-making that do materialise are just as transient: media-led public outcries are merely Brussels Choiach.

41 See in particular *Euro Puppets: The European Commission's Remaking of Civil Society*, Chris Snowdon, IEA, 2013; plus *The Hard Sell: EU Communication Policy and the Campaign for Hearts and Minds*, Rotherham/Mullally, 2008.

Chapter 7

1 Found in the web archive, http://web.archive.org/web/20120120083358/http://www.taxpayersalliance.com/termsofendearment.pdf

2 On 'rubber articles' see earlier. Passerelles allow for voting mechanisms in the treaties to shift without a new treaty (and can include loss of the veto). The term is the French word for a connecting bridge, such as the Bridge of Sighs in Venice, and equally appropriately it also happens to be the nautical term used for a gangplank.

3 Conversely, one is reminded of Romano Prodi's rejoinder on the way you could rename a putative European army something else to make it more palatable; and similarly the manner in which the title of European Constitution was dropped but the overwhelming bulk of clauses survived as the Treaty of Lisbon.

4 Subsequent policy papers proposed areas of actual negotiating focus, for instance November 2013 with *Mandate for Reform*. These are, however, broad brush and should equally be considered in the context of the traffic light system.

NOTES

5   Published by the author in earlier works, but also in the handbook so included here.

6   Or indeed Metropolitan France and then the informal legacy agreements encompassing Algeria (1957-1980s), though leading in the reverse direction in terms of political assimilation. The case histories of both East Berlin and Algiers are worthy of study in their own right. Category 0 status here refers to their condition and status under assimilated sovereignty though.

7   'Sir John Major: UK wouldn't have an NHS without migrants', BBC website, 16 November 2014.

8   The Commission does not distinguish in its categorisation between opt-out states and others; this would accept the principle that such divisions are enduring.

9   See http://www.economy.gov.tr/index.cfm?sayfa=tradeagreements&bolum=fta&region=0

10 See http://ec.europa.eu/trade/policy/countries-and-regions/agreements/#_europe

11 The logic follows that if we are pessimistic about the FCO's likelihood of ever using them to defend the national interest, we must rule out EEA membership as an option.

12 See http://www.tfa.net/wp-content/uploads/2014/10/ManningThePumps.pdf
    The Goldilocks Zone is part of a planet's possible orbit that's neither too hot nor too cold for life, but just right. A similar principle is applied to treaty terms, between assimilation and economic distance beyond any gravitational action.

13 Any unduly nervous Whitehall reader could simply replace this phrase with that of 'having left the current EU treaties' to achieve an equally meaningful end result.

14 We differ from some commentators by putting more emphasis on the EEA as a default resting point if renegotiation falters, recognising the complexities involved (it may even turn out to resemble a 'reverse accession', with chapters concluded individually: our more complex trade arrangements will need to be parked somewhere while these are being finalised - see the TFA paper referenced subsequently). We are slightly less dismissive though than some other commentators about the IEA competition having had no strategic success other than embarrassing the FCO overnight and buying someone a piano. For one thing, the competition inspired the TFA paper (which was not submitted as it followed a different set of starting principles that it identified as more important to address).

15 *UK Policy Options if it Leaves the EU*, May 2014. Again, for nervous Whitehall Warriors, replace 'leave' with 'rethink' and the end consequence and destination can remain the same.

16 *Setting Out the British Option: Liberating 95% of Businesses from EU Red Tape* (2014)

17 Article 50 constitutes both a two year stopwatch for finishing the renegotiations, and a formal trigger. On the (perhaps presumptuous) assumption that any new treaty could have a relatively swift introduction date stated as part of it, Article 50 might then need only be triggered if the talks themselves stalled. The matter is a balance of impetus against transitional continuity. But it should not be dismissed out of hand.

18 Sir Con O'Neill during the original accession negotiations had told colleagues that the *acquis* was non-negotiable, that they should just accept it and move on: 'Swallow it whole and swallow it now' (see Booker and North, *The Great Deception*). This was a defeatist approach necessitated by having a governmental policy that prioritised accession over price. It has marred FCO strategy since.

19 The document has been released online by the Ukraine Government, and summaries also exist including one by the Commission and another by the Konrad Adenauer Stiftung.

20 The statistics are unclear and estimates vary. This can be attributed to different time frames under consideration, complications arising from counting local equivalents to SIs, and masked origin. See *Controversies*, http://web.archive.org/web/20130725010016/http://www.taxpayersalliance.com/controversies.pdf

21 Particularly the Bruges Group research 'EFTA or EU?' (Hugo Van Randwyck) and 'The Norway Option' (Dr Richard North). Also one chapter in Controversies (Dr Lee Rotherham, EU Referendum Campaign; online at TPA- see earlier).

23 *20 Years Of The European Single Market: Growth Effects of EU Integration,* Future Social Market Economy, 2014

24 Sweden's gain is not surprising when one considers that the Federal Museum in Bonn (Geschichte der Bundesrepublik Deutschland) has a telling display of FRG imports c. 1957. Swedish imports exceeded those of France, and not simply because of ore. Both countries trade were dwarfed not by the UK (which was lower still) but by the Netherlands, followed by Belgium's. The influence of the Rhineland economy in driving EU integration cannot be understated.

25 *Where's The Insider Advantage? A Comparative Study of UK Exports to EU and Non-EU Nations Between 1960 and 2012,* Michael Burrage, Civitas, 2014

26 *Withdrawal From the EU Would Not Damage Our Car Industry: True or False?* (Civitas, 2013). This includes a number of useful tables reviewing the key manufacturers as well as national comparisons.

27 I.e. issues which no one has thought of yet. Likely to be an important list.

28 Bismarck (actually, a doubtful attribution) may have likened law making to sausage manufacture as something the electorate should not see. European law making has the added complexities of a paella factory run by a dysfunctional cooperative.

29 It is a measure of how matters have progressed and accelerated over the last two decades that if John Major had ended up with Maastricht from the negotiating starting point of Lisbon, he would likely today be lauded as a Eurosceptic Jove.

30 Plus the Dutch, Poles, to a degree the Italians, the Scandinavians (including non-EU Norway) and certain other contingents depending on national interests.

31 We are not so cruel after radical renegotiation as to seek to introduce to the European Parliament another West Lothian Question. In any case, given the constituencies and for balance, we might style it the South East England Question instead.

32 Given their loyalties lie with the Commission and not to member states, coupled with their sub-proportional numbers, and the presence of a number of angry unions representing them, we would anticipate UK employees being encouraged to retire and no new intake being recruited rather than there being mass sackings. The Commissioner as a political appointee would probably be alone in not being protected by contract. Given the inevitable pay offs and pensions, it is not an issue Whitehall frankly need expend political capital on. Instead it should focus on the massive liabilities arising from the existing pensions black hole covering EU staff, as well as the UK share of physical assets.

33 I.e. before the fall of the Berlin Wall and the introduction of a mobile, low-paid, Anglophone, extremely large, and, it must be said, comparatively highly motivated workforce.

34 The EEC first established a Common External Tariff in 1968, in tandem with removing internal tariffs. At an external average of 10.4%, it provided an obvious incentive for the UK to apply for membership of the customs union, particularly as it had averaged German tariffs upwards. However, just as the UK joined, the Kennedy Round derogation was already running out, which had the effect of pushing average EEC external rates down to 6.6%. This, coupled with the fact that the UK had been quite protectionist at the time, suggests that one undeclared reason why the Heath government pushed accession was more to permanently cut its own rates (and hence, end protectionist domestic attitudes) rather than in order to reduce tariffs on UK exports imposed by anyone else. If so, it has worked, and we can now move on.

NOTES

35 See the OECD's *The European Union's Trade Policies and their Economic Effects* (2000), UN Comtrade and IMF figures, and the WTO website. The work done by the Trade Policy Research Centre is extremely valuable in reviewing what this means. By means of comparison with these tariffs, UK businesses manage to profitably trade into the US market at an average 3.48% bound, Canada 6.82%, Australia 9.95%, China 10.02%, and India 48.55%. We might further add that the £2.55bn estimate itself includes Rotterdam/Antwerp distortion, so a more likely figure would be around £2.3bn.

36 The EU's bound tariff list runs to 5,119 subheadings at last count, while other key WTO material relating to ongoing bilateral negotiations is classified as 'Secret', which is why the detailed Treasury study is required.

37 The question of third party treaty inheritance is a complex one deserving of detailed study in its own right. The Scottish referendum threw up some interesting notions in particular. The basic lessons learned over the past 40 years appear to be that treaties are treated by countersignatories as passed on to successor states so long as everyone is still happy with them; and that the prospect of lapsing into 'chaos at midnight' trumps individual concerns. This assumes that relative voting balance over an issue of current contention is not upset by the creation of an additional seat.

38 Whitehall during the Constitutional Convention naturally focused on the Labour Government's priorities of reviewing additional powers as they were being placed on the table by others. It was left to 'dissidents' to generate a Minority Report suggesting the reverse.